Coriolanus

William Shakespeare

Guide written by
Stewart Martin

Charles Letts & Co Ltd
London, Edinburgh & New York

First published 1988
by Charles Letts & Co Ltd
Diary House, Borough Road, London SE1 1DW

Illustration: Peter McClure

This series of literature guides has been
conceived and developed by John Mahoney and
Stewart Martin

Stewart Martin is an Honours graduate of Lancaster University, where he read English
and Sociology. He has worked both in the UK and abroad as a teacher, an educational
consultant, and a writer. He is married with three children, and is currently Deputy
Headteacher at Ossett School in West Yorkshire.

John Mahoney has taught English for twenty years. He has been head of the English
department in three schools and has wide experience of preparing students at all levels
for most examination boards. He has worked both in the UK and North America
producing educational books and computer software on English language and literature.
He is married with three children and lives in Worcestershire.

British Library Cataloguing in Publication Data
Martin, Stewart
Coriolanus, William Shakespeare.—
(Guides to literature)
1. Drama in English. Shakespeare, William,
1564–1616. Coriolanus. Study outlines
I. Title   II. Shakespeare, William, 1564–1616. Coriolanus
III. Series 822.3'3

ISBN 0 85097 843 2

Printed and bound in Great Britain by
Charles Letts (Scotland) Ltd

Contents

To the student

An especially important aspect of any study of literature is that you should reach your *own* views about whatever novel, poem or play you are studying, and be able to quote examples from the text to support these views. Your quotations need not be lengthy, but they must be pertinent. Your views need not be orthodox, nor need they accord with those of eminent critics, who in any case are sometimes in violent disagreement with each other.

The temptation simply to 'parrot' the views of others must be firmly resisted, especially if you are unclear about, or are out of sympathy with, their sentiments. This is not always as easy for students as is sometimes made out, but nonetheless, teachers, assessors and examination boards are looking for evidence of your ability to express your own understanding and insight. This does not, of course, mean that you are forbidden to hold similar views to any of those expressed by critics. It will be taken for granted that you have done your background reading about the author's time, and have studied the established critical opinions, but you need to show that you have done something more with all this information than simply learned it.

You should be clear in your own mind about your answers to the questions incorporated in the commentary text. It would be a good idea to make your own notes for each one, detailing the essential points you would make in a coursework essay or examination answer. Such questions will not have definitive answers, so you should not be worried if you are uncertain as to the truth of the matter. If you have contradicting impressions, then admit it, set them down clearly, with evidence, and try to reach an overall conclusion. Your views may sometimes end up being of the 'on balance' type – do not worry, this is to be expected, and is perfectly normal. Remember: the play is not a jigsaw-puzzle or a murder-mystery which you are expected somehow to 'solve'; it is a great literary work, to which you are expected to make an intelligent, informed, sensitive and individual response.

William Shakespeare

His name is protean. He begets doubles at every corner. His penmanship is unconsciously faked by lawyers who happen to write a similar hand. On the wet morning of November 27, 1582, he is Shaxpere and she is Wately of Temple Grafton. A couple of days later he is Shagspere and she is Hathway of Stratford-on-Avon.

Vladimir Nabokov (from *Bend Sinister*)

Attempts to find out much about William Shakespeare seem doomed to failure at worst, and frustration at best. The literature on this topic is vast, but the reliable facts are few and far between, and sometimes contradictory from one source to another. At times it seems easier to identify what we do *not* know about Shakespeare, than what we do. Nothing can be gleaned from his plays about Shakespeare the man, and a typical reference to contemporary affairs – such as the riot over the shortage of corn which opens *Coriolanus* and which can be related to contemporary riots over the price of food – will tell us nothing about his views on such matters. The allegedly autobiographical core of material in his sonnets is maddeningly enigmatic, and could in fact be evidence of the author's supreme art – the creation of the illusion that we can see into his heart and mind. For all practical purposes, we have to admit that Shakespeare the individual is well-nigh invisible.

Sources are vague about exactly where or when Shakespeare was born. We know that Mary Shakespeare had her third child christened on 26 April 1564, but after that there is an historical silence about him for almost twenty years. We know that his literary contemporaries were well-schooled, and that, for example, Marlowe, Greene and Nash went to Cambridge, Jonson was at Westminster School, Middleton and Chapman went to Oxford, Kyd went to Merchant Taylors' School, and so on. But we have no evidence that Shakespeare ever went to school at all or, if he did, where it was; and it is doubtful if either of his parents could read or write. Shakespeare's daughter, Judith, was so illiterate she could not even write her own name.

Shakespeare's marriage is part of the folklore surrounding him, but in fact we do not know definitely whom he married, or where he married, or even when he married. The register of licences has an entry for November 27, 1582, giving the bride's name as Anne Whateley of Temple Grafton. It seems odd that this could have been confused with the entry for the following day, when a £40 bond was provided, and where the woman's name is given as Anne Hathaway of Stratford. Given that Anne Hathaway had Susanna Shakespeare christened on May 26, 1583, she must have been pregnant at the time of marriage. Some scholars have argued that the Hathaway family must have applied pressure to cancel Shakespeare's intended marriage to Anne Whateley; others that Anne Whateley never existed, and the confusion is more imagined than real, the matter being a clerical mix-up. The truth remains elusive. Between the christening of his children and his rise to theatrical fame in London there are the 'lost' years of Shakespeare: for the seven years between 1585 and 1592 nothing whatsoever is known about him.

Writing in the eighteenth century, George Steevens made what is still quite possibly the definitive biographical statement on the subject:

All that is known with any degree of certainty concerning Shakespeare is that he was born in Stratford-upon-Avon, married and had children there, went to London where . . . he wrote poems and plays, returned to Stratford, made his will, died, and was buried.

Of the six known signatures of Shakespeare, no two are the same, although in fairness we must remember that this was not unusual in his day. No play has even been found written in his own hand; and nothing in his will suggests that he ever wrote poetry or drama. None of the contemporary Stratford records which mention him ever alludes to his being a playwright or poet. Why he should be so indifferent to the fate of his work is not known.

In summary, not much is known for certain about Shakespeare's private life, and it matters little for the enjoyment of his plays. He seems to have started writing plays under his own name in about 1591. He was a prolific writer, and within two or three years he had produced several comedies and histories, as well as a sort of horror tragedy. Compared with the work of previous playwrights, these early plays were outstanding for their style and characterization, but for Shakespeare they were merely an apprenticeship for his later work.

Shakespeare was not concerned with originality of plot, nor did his audience expect it; Biblical stories, legends and histories were the basis of most plays of the time. *Coriolanus* is set in Rome, Corioles, Antium and their environs, because that is where the original story was set, but the setting would be of little interest to Shakespeare's audience. It is doubtful if many, or indeed any, would have visited Italy, and they neither wanted nor expected accuracy of detail. The social background of the play is that of England in the late-sixteenth century and the citizens with their clubs in the first scene could easily have been London apprentices about to join in a fight.

Elizabethan society

The population of England increased during the sixteenth century, from about two-and-a-half million at the beginning, to perhaps four million by the end. This may have been due to the dying out of the bubonic plague, which had ravaged the mid-fourteenth century population, reducing it by about a quarter, and still caused many deaths in London in bad years. Smallpox, which was to ravage the seventeenth century, had not yet reached its peak. As the population grew, food prices rose, but there was no comparable rise in wages since the market was full of people looking for work. The poor became poorer, finally seeking work in towns. Towns were growing, thanks to a growth in trade. London grew fastest, from about 50,000 inhabitants to 200,000 by the end of the century.

Unfortunately this growth tended to concentrate and magnify the effects of disease. In 1625 more than 40,000 people died in London – 1 in 8 of the whole population. Plague victims died in the streets, in the fields and outside the houses of countryfolk, who barricaded themselves in. Most of those who found work in town wisely left their families behind in the country, as did Shakespeare. Food riots were the usual result of bad times, with people taking to the roads as refugees. Food riots are mentioned several times in *Coriolanus*. The concentration of large numbers of the dispossessed and wretched, together with a lack of sanitation, made the towns dirty, smelly, crowded and unhealthy. The epithets which Coriolanus flings repeatedly at the plebeians may have been perceived by the Elizabethan audience as slightly less inflammatory than we find them.

Religion preoccupied people intensely in the half century from 1580. Although drama was not supposed to concern itself with contentious questions, especially concerning religion, or even to name God at all, nevertheless tragic drama did have a lot to say about death – the spirit in which men encountered it, and the variety of means to achieve it. Coriolanus is outraged that his soldiers have their hurts 'behind', for this means they were gained whilst running away from the enemy. Much is also made in *Coriolanus* of the warrior-codes of battle and the virtue which accrues from honouring them.

The Elizabethan age was a fascinating mixture of great religious zeal, hypocrisy and intolerance. For example, Bishop Hooper, who visited the Gloucester diocese in 1551, was furious to discover that of 311 clergymen he saw, 168 did not know the Ten Commandments, 39 had no idea where the Lord's Prayer was to be found in the Bible, 34 did not know its author and 10 could not even remember it.

By the time of Shakespeare the Church had fallen into disrepute, with people worshipping certain saints for particular kinds of protection, buying pardons for sins, saying prayers to offset punishments, giving money for masses to be recited for them and for other kinds of 'insurance'. Relics, pardons and the use of charms to ward off evil had helped depress faith to the level of superstition. Seeing the world in terms of an endless struggle between the powers of good and evil encouraged people to believe in things like witchcraft, the idea of 'good' days and of good or bad luck. In *Coriolanus* we see a pagan notion of the 'wheel of fortune' implicit in the drama – a man raises himself up to a height of pride, and is then humbled by a fall to insignificance or death.

This fall parallels the Christian version of the Fall of the angels, and was seen as the process by which man learned the Christian virtue of humility. The section of *Coriolanus* where the warrior is unable to don the robe of humility and beg for the citizens' 'voices' would therefore have had considerable significance for Shakespeare's audience.

Coriolanus, however, does not present us with an unambiguous case of pride; we do not know how far, in Christian terms, he is ripe for being punished with a lesson in humiliation. Coriolanus rejects rewards for his achievements, he refuses the spoils of war, and he does not want to be consul. The question is whether Coriolanus's pride is an assumed or natural characteristic – if assumed, we may deem it ambition, if natural we may have to account it nobility. As has been pointed out by several critics, the characters who accuse Coriolanus of pride reveal as much about themselves by so doing, as they reveal about him.

Coriolanus's relationships with the other members of his family are based upon the conventions prevailing in Elizabethan family life. Although the most passionate arguments of the age were about the nature and extent of the power of God and King, 'Honour thy father and thy mother' was a Commandment which was treated with the utmost seriousness. Upper class society expected elaborate displays of deference to parents, like sons doffing their hats and daughters kneeling or standing in the presence of their parents. For most people, their children were their only monuments to the future, and, especially in an age of high infant death rates, it was a cause of bitter disappointment to have none. Sons especially were important, for it was through them that family property and titles descended – hence the struggles of Henry VIII to have a son.

It was customary for children to kneel each morning before their parents to ask for blessing, and to do the same on arrival and departure from home – the latter even when grown up. This would give powerful emphasis to the issues raised, for example, in *King Lear*, and would place Coriolanus's kneeling to his mother in an understood context. Other things, however, would have been less familiar to Shakespeare's audience. For example, women had no property rights until 300 years after Shakespeare's death, and within a typical Elizabethan family women were subservient to all men, including boys over the age of seven. The status of Volumnia in *Coriolanus* would therefore have occasioned much interest, perhaps especially as England had in its Queen an equally shrewd and politically astute woman, who was also not without steel.

There was a clear social order in England at this time, with an insistence on the observance of 'degree, priority and place'. At the top was the monarch, then came the nobility. In Elizabeth's time there were only about 60 peers, and they held tremendous power. Only their heirs could inherit the title, any other male children merely being accorded the status of 'gentleman'.

The Court of Queen Elizabeth was the focus of intellectual life and achievement, and she surrounded herself with men of talent. To these men she gave great power, and in return they put a great deal of energy into giving the Queen lavish hospitality when she visited their houses, and also gave her many gifts. There are many significant parallels between the Elizabethan structure of government and that of ancient Rome.

The peers formed the House of Lords in Parliament, and like their Roman equivalent the patricians, held most of the leading positions in government, army and diplomatic functions. The House of Commons in Parliament was recognized as the voice of the English people as a whole, as was the Roman Senate. However, just as the Elizabethan Parliament was summoned at the whim of the monarch and could as easily be dismissed, so the patricians could remove from the plebeians the tribunes who represented them. It was some time before Parliament gained any real power in England, and the gentlemen landowners effectively ruled the countryside. They were appointed by the Crown as Justices of the Peace, and were responsible, under a judge, for the exercise of justice in their areas. Justices of the Peace could also fix local wages and prices, regulate trade and enforce laws, very loosely paralleling the rights and responsibilities of the Consuls of Rome. They were also responsible for overseeing the parish officers, who dealt with all the local problems at village level. The parish was effectively the unit of local government. Within it, a constable was expected to keep good order, catch any criminals and carry out such punishments as whipping convicted criminals.

In the third scene of Act three in *Coriolanus,* the tribunes, in talking about the structure of the Roman State, mention the 'strength o'th'commons', they talk about polls and 'tribes', and an allusion is made to voting. These closely parallel the system in Elizabethan England, where the election of the House of Commons was similar. Understandably, Shakespeare couched his descriptions of the political machinery of the Roman State in terms which would be familiar to his audience. It would, however, not have escaped Shakespeare's notice that, apart from the Roman State having no head other than that of a Hydra, there were many similarities – indeed there continue to be many similarities. One of the remarkable achievements of the play is that its political debate is so framed that it has relevance for all political systems today.

The Elizabethan age

The problem we have with understanding the Elizabethan view of the world, or indeed any view of the world from a different time or culture, is that so much of it is taken for granted; just as we take our own view of the world for granted now. Phrases such as 'the iron curtain', 'to boldly go', 'mission aborted', 'continental drift', 'expanding universe', and so on, fill our language. We have no trouble recognizing the context of phrases like these, and we can use them in our normal conversation. We can even make jokes which rely on such knowledge for their impact. So it has always been in any culture.

One of the problems which we all have with understanding other people is working out not so much what they are *saying,* but rather what they *mean.* This is harder when they are from another culture, more difficult when that culture no longer exists, and even worse when dealing with literature. Works of literature always assume a lot of background knowledge on the part of the reader; writers do not normally write their material for future generations, but for their own. We are not usually so aware of these assumptions in the literature of our own time, but they are very obvious to us, for example, in Shakespeare's plays. An additional factor is that the plays were written to be watched, rather than read: they were not written as novels, to be 'acted out' in the reader's mind, but were intended to be seen as continuous action.

Many of the ideas which the Elizabethans had may strike us as extremely odd – for instance, the idea that God put the element of air between the heavenly element of fire and the earthly element of water to stop them fighting, and that, whilst angels take their form from the interplanetary ether, devils take theirs from the muddy air of earth. It is difficult for us to imagine a world in which such ideas were commonplace.

In the Elizabethan age there were many different opinions about the way the universe was made up, although both the Church and the Court held in common a mass of assumptions: for instance, that the Earth was unmoving, in the centre of the universe, and everything (Sun, Moon, stars and so on) went around it. This was actually a simplified version of an older and much more complicated medieval idea, which saw the universe as highly organized, arranged in a series of levels of greater or lesser importance. These 'hierarchies' included every object, person and thing in the universe: everything had its own place in these hierarchies. Everything fitted in somewhere, and was connected (through the hierarchies) to everything else, rather like a vast and complicated three-dimensional jigsaw puzzle.

Although they knew of the ideas of Copernicus, they were reluctant to have their ideas about the 'fixed' universe upset. Like most people, they probably preferred a tidy, organized system they understood, to a new idea, one which pushed the Earth from the centre of the universe to a place on its edge. The medieval and Elizabethan view of the world and the universe was based on the idea that everything was constructed by God for the benefit and use of man. Everything (literally) revolved around man.

To us the idea of 'chaos' means only confusion, a large-scale mess, something completely unorganized. To the Elizabethans, however, it meant the total destruction of everything which existed before the Creation. The Elizabethans thought that the universe existed only because of man. Man had free choice about what he did. Everything else was fixed in its hierarchy, occupying its own place. Man could change the world if he wished, but he had been given it by God to look after. So the Elizabethans had strong views on responsibility – man was under a duty to exercise care and protection of the world, and through it, the universe. If man did not keep everything in order, the law of nature would stop operating. If the law of nature stopped working, then chaos would return to the universe, and everything would be destroyed.

We can see many references to chaos in Shakespeare's works, and some characters in his plays are preoccupied with the idea – Othello, for example. The idea runs through many of his other plays too, like *Julius Caesar, King Lear, Macbeth* and *Coriolanus*. This whole approach is radically different to some modern thinking, which argues that man is insignificant, and that the universe is unaware of his existence, and would continue perfectly well without him if he disappeared tomorrow.

There was an idea in the Middle Ages (from roughly 1000 AD to the fifteenth century), originating with the astronomer Ptolemy, that certain types of people are associated with certain planets. People who used fire (blacksmiths, cooks, etc.) were thought to be associated with the Sun, and with Mars, the mythical god of fire and war. This system was highly complicated, and eventually became too convoluted to remain coherent. Nevertheless, the system survived, and we can see evidence of it in many of Shakespeare's plays. In *Twelfth Night* we can see the medieval idea that parts of the body were associated with different parts of the heavens:

SIR TOBY BELCH:	I did think by the excellent constitution of thy leg it was formed under the star of a galliard.
SIR ANDREW AGUECHEEK:	Ay, 'tis strong, and it does indifferently well in a flame-coloured stock. Shall we set about some revels?
SIR TOBY:	What shall we do else? Were we not born under Taurus?
SIR ANDREW:	Taurus: that's sides and heart.
SIR TOBY:	No, sir, it is legs and thighs.

This is a joke, as Shakespeare almost certainly knew that Taurus was in fact associated with the neck and throat. Sir Toby is therefore right, in a way he did not mean – he meant that their revels should be dancing (legs and thighs), but the neck and throat would suggest drinking.

One of the amazing things about the Elizabethan age is that it managed to include so much that was new, without really abandoning anything of the old. For example in *Macbeth* there is a scene which refers to the healing powers of the English King; this was an idea relating to the notion of a cosmic order, the medieval 'hierarchy' system.

The Elizabethans also retained some other ideas from the Middle Ages, like their views on sin and salvation: for them the most vital part of the Bible was not about the life of Christ – important though that was – but the fall of the bad angels, the creation, the temptation of man, and his salvation through the coming of Christ.

The 'ladder of creation' or 'chain of being' was the way in which everything was arranged in order, from the nearest to God to the farthest away. Every speck in the universe was a link in the chain somewhere, and all the links were connected without a gap.

At the bottom of the chain of being were the elements, metals and liquids. Even here, discrete links in the chain are present – water is nobler than earth, gold is nobler than lead, and so on. Next came things that had life, like plants, with some higher up the chain (or ladder) than others – the oak was nobler than the nettle, for example. Next came things with feelings, split into three classes – first the things with touch, but no hearing, memory or movement (e.g., shellfish), second the things with touch, memory and movement but no hearing (e.g., ants), third the things with all these attributes (e.g., horses, cats). These three classes led up to man, who had everything that all the others below him had, plus the faculty of understanding. Because the chain was also thought of as a ladder, there was the possibility of movement up and down. For example, plants might feed the animals, and the animals might be used as food by man.

As the Elizabethans saw it, the main function of all the non-human things in the chain of being was to give man examples of how he should behave and conduct himself. For instance, the ants were wonderful in themselves, but were there mainly to show the lazy person how he should work. Similarly the bees were incredibly well organized, but their main function was to remind man that order should prevail in society under the rule of the King. Every aspect of everything was interconnected in this way, and nature thus became God's moral textbook for man, so that by studying it he could strive to become closer to God.

Everything had its place, and everything had its own particular characteristics which made it admirable in some respect or other. For instance, stones may have been below plants on the ladder, but they exceeded them in strength and lifetime. Plants may not have feelings, but they excel at assimilating nourishment. The animals are stronger than man. Man excels the angels in his power of learning. The angels cannot rise beyond their place in the chain, for they are dedicated to the adoration of that which is above them. Within each class of things on the ladder of Creation, there was also thought to be one supreme thing on the border with the next class, for example, the dolphin among fishes, the eagle among birds, the lion among beasts and the King (or Emperor) among men. There was sometimes a difference of opinion about these examples, but never about the last one given, the primacy of the sovereign. Other examples were the primacy of God among the angels, the Sun among the stars, justice among the virtues, and the head among the parts of the body. This last example is apparent in *Coriolanus* in the fable of the belly, and has important connotations for the action of the play, where the ancient republic of Rome, having overthrown its monarch, struggles to survive in a situation where the body politic is without its 'head'.

Shakespeare was always concerned with the general notion of order, and in *The Tempest* we see him concerned with the chain of being itself. Macbeth's discussion about what kind of men the murderers are is a good example – he lists all the kinds of creature which may be called 'dogs', but points out that although they are all in the chain of being, those at the bottom of the list of dogs may not be equated with those at the top.

In *Coriolanus*, the opening scenes concerning the mob's insurrection would have struck a powerful chord in the audience. This would have had special relevance because of the contemporary enclosures of common lands by rich farmers who wanted more pastures for their sheep. In 1607, for example, there were several outbreaks of civil unrest in the Midland counties connected with this very issue. The vandalism and disorder were described as the most violent for many years. It would therefore seem eminently reasonable to the Elizabethans that Coriolanus berate the citizenry who carry 'staves, clubs and other weapons', and characterize them in a denigrating way with images of sickness, disease and inconstancy.

There are a great number of references to the 'elements', or 'humours' in Shakespeare's works, where they serve to link the doings of men with the workings of the universe. The four elements – Earth, Water, Air, Fire – were also basic to the study of alchemy, where gold was deemed the king of metals, and a permanent, perfect mixture of the elements. The same mixture in man produced perfect health. Gold was unique on earth and nothing known to the Elizabethans could damage, dissolve or destroy it in any way.

Like everything else, man was made of the four elements, although in him they were called 'humours': Melancholy, Phlegm, Blood, Choler. These fluid humours were related to the four elements, and a proper mixture of them was needed for growth and health. The fable of the belly in *Coriolanus* would have struck a powerful chord in the minds of the audience, for the Elizabethans thought that food was made of the four elements, and when eaten went through the stomach to the liver. The liver then made four liquids, and these were the four humours. The humours generated heat, and this so-called 'vital heat' was spread through the body by 'spirits'. Some of these spirits were in the form of a vapour, and were formed in the liver and carried along the veins with the humours.

When the humours and spirits reached the heart they were acted upon by heat and air from the lungs, and were changed to 'vital spirits'. The heart also made a 'nobler' kind of blood, and it was this noble blood which, together with the vital spirits, carried life and heat through the arteries to the rest of the body. The heart was the seat of the passions and was king of the middle part of the body. Because of its role in making the four humours, the liver was king of the lower part of the body. It is to these things that the belly refers in Menenius's fable, which talks of how the 'members' receive from it 'that natural competency/Whereby they live'.

Some of the vital spirits went to what the belly calls 'th'seat o'th'brain', where they were turned into 'animal spirits'. The animal spirits worked through the nerves to tell the body what the brain needed, and were connected both to the body and to the soul. The brain was the king of the top part of the body. This is the part which in Shakespeare's ancient Rome was missing, being replaced by a 'many-headed monster'.

Most Elizabethans would have been quite comfortable with the idea that the head was the noblest part of the body, because it was nearest the heavens, and the heart was the source of light and vigour because it was in the middle of the body, as the Sun was in the 'middle' of the planets.

At the end of *Julius Caesar* we see Antony telling the crowd that Brutus was a perfectly balanced man, in whom the humours were correctly mixed. In *Coriolanus* we find Menenius telling everyone what a 'humorous patrician' he is. Usually in people one humour was more prominent than the others, which is what gave them their own individual characters. In abnormal circumstances the humours might not spread in the natural fashion; it was thought that they could rise from the abdomen straight to the brain as a vapour. Catarrh was thought to result from this kind of thing. Given the headless state of Rome which we find in *Coriolanus*, the Elizabethans would have probably expected the State to fall prey to ill-humours, and would have found the sickness and disease imagery which runs through the play very appropriate.

The Elizabethans placed great emphasis on what they saw as man's two unique characteristics, his understanding and his free will. They felt that man begins in ignorance and must be educated towards the angels. But not only must man learn about God, he must learn about himself, or he is no better than the beasts. 'Knowing yourself' was the key to virtue, because it was thought that man's greatest enemy was within himself, and he must learn to know his enemy if he was to defeat it. Both Othello and King Lear are defective in understanding, just as Hamlet and Macbeth are defective in will. Coriolanus's virtue is that, throughout the play, the only character who understands him is himself. In several senses we might feel that Coriolanus is 'constant' throughout the play, and what changes is our perception of him, as illuminated through the eyes of other characters and the names they give him.

The Elizabethan interest in the nature of man was intense, and Shakespeare explored it to the full – not just through the actions of his characters, but through the themes and images which are woven into his works. He used these to explore man's relationship with heaven, with hell, with the beasts and the universe at large.

In *Hamlet* we see man depicted 'in action how like an angel, in apprehension how like a god'. Yet in *Macbeth* we see man capable of extremes of base behaviour. Macbeth's sin is not only against human decency, but against the whole chain of being, as is often pointed up by the imagery of animals and beasts.

Man's simultaneous greatness and littleness, acted out as a kind of drama in this world, was a constant theme of the literature of the age, and pride was counted a crucial weakness in man. Man's fall from grace had weakened his understanding, as well as corrupting his will, and made him his own worst enemy in his attempt to be reunited with God. This explains the frequent battle in many of Shakespeare's tragic heroes between their reason and their feelings or, in the case of Coriolanus, between virtue and pride.

It was a common Elizabethan notion that the order in the State duplicated the order in the universe. This is the central theme of several of Shakespeare's plays, notably *Macbeth* and *King Lear*. Frequent comparisons were made between the King, ruler of the State, and the Sun, ruler of the heavens. Similarly, disorder in the heavens paralleled civil disorder in the State. Some of the best-known episodes in Shakespeare's plays deal with this point – for example the descriptions of natural chaos that follow the deaths of Caesar in *Julius Caesar*, or of Duncan in *Macbeth*. King Lear in the storm also gives us the best-known example of the connection between the passions of man and the storms in the elements. We call this supposed relationship the 'pathetic fallacy', and it is equally important in the study of later Romantic poets, like Wordsworth ('pathos' meaning to have feelings in sympathy with another, and 'fallacy' because the whole idea is misleading).

Also common to the age was the perception of an order in the world of the beasts and plants, which reflected the order in the rest of the universe. The Elizabethans classified the animal kingdom into four groups; beasts, fowl, fish, and creeping things. Most knowledge about animals was derived from folklore from everyday country life, or from books written by travellers. The kinds of domesticated and wild animals in Elizabethan England seem to have been much as they are now, for although wolves still ran wild in Scotland and Ireland, the wild boars and wild bulls which Shakespeare sometimes mentions had long since vanished. The fox, the badger, the otter, the rabbit, the hare, and the weasel were all hunted as vermin, along with all other wild mammals.

Some Elizabethan notions about animals were very similar to our modern ones: for example that the serpent is base and wicked, and that the lion is fierce and noble. The lion would never hurt 'the true prince' (*Henry IV*, Part 1): it could recognize the true king by his nobility. It was also thought never to eat dead meat (carrion). Coriolanus refers to Aufidius as 'a lion that I am proud to hunt'. Some of the other ideas which the Elizabethans had were influenced by accounts from abroad (often garbled), errors of understanding, and their powerful contemporary mythology. Shakespeare does not mention all the beliefs about animals common to his time, but he uses quite a large number of them, and over seventy references occur in *Coriolanus*.

In Shakespeare's day there were many legends about what we now think were completely mythical animals, although their names have sometimes been used for actual creatures which were discovered later–like the pelican and salamander. Reptiles, crawling things and insects were thought of as being 'creepy' and horrible, toads were regarded as poisonous things which 'live upon the vapour of a dungeon' (*Othello*), and spiders were thought to suck poison up from the earth.

The animal references in *Coriolanus* are mostly negative in the characteristics which they ascribe. For example, the plebeians are at various times denigrated as 'curs' and 'dogs', or are described as 'beasts' and 'monsters'. Shakespeare commonly used references to classes of animals in this way to highlight the defects of particular examples–thus in *Macbeth* the hero lists the different kinds of dog as 'hounds and greyhounds, mongrels, spaniels, curs, shoughs, water-rugs, and demi-wolves'; and makes the apt comment that if in such a 'catalogue' all these are 'dogs', then maybe the murderers could be 'men'. Coriolanus uses most of these examples to characterize the plebeians, although he speaks of Titus Lartius–a fellow patrician and general–as a 'greyhound' about to be unleashed, for not all dogs were deemed to be equally noble, and this was equally true of men.

Imagery of feeding, of mouths, tongues and the body is extended from the corn riots at the start of the play, when Coriolanus notes that 'The Volsces have much corn' and invites the tribunes to gather the plebeians together and 'take these rats thither'. Ironically, rats always left a doomed ship. The 'rat without a tail' mentioned in *Macbeth* (Act three, scene one) could be a guinea-pig, but probably refers to something else: the idea that, although witches would change shape into animals when they wanted, they could never do it exactly. Slightly imperfect animals were often killed by the Elizabethans, because they thought they were transformed witches.

The Elizabethans saw all creatures made from mixtures of different animals as particularly evil, and a lot of their monsters were invented this way; the bat, for example, was deemed to be an animal of the devil, because it was thought to be an unnatural mixture of a bird's wings and a mouse's teeth. Notice how Coriolanus describes the plebeians as a 'multiplying spawn' of 'monsters', as Hydra-headed mixtures of witless geese, carrion crows, as camels and asses fit only to bear burdens, as savage apes and the like. However, Coriolanus himself is described several times as an unnatural figure, as an 'engine', as a 'thing made by some other deity than nature', as a serpent and a 'dragon'.

All worms, serpents and snakes were thought to sting with their tongues. Adders were thought to be deaf, and their young were thought to chew their way out of the sides of their mother. Coriolanus is dubbed 'viperous' by Sicinius, 'dragon-like' by Aufidius, and 'more than a creeping thing' by Menenius. Dragons, whose lairs were caves, were thought to be of two kinds, those with, and those without, wings and many stories existed about how they and their hated enemies–elephants–would fight to destroy each other. Other, related, great monsters called leviathans were thought to exist in the sea, a reference derived from ancient Hebrew poetry.

The metaphors of snakes, dragons and worms which surround Coriolanus connect interestingly with other allusions to do with his wish to make himself a new name out of the fire 'of burning Rome': the salamander was a kind of lizard which could live in fire and the phoenix, of which there was only ever one, made its home in the deserts of Arabia and lived for hundreds of years, during which time it regularly built a nest and burnt itself to death, to arise reborn from its own ashes.

The basilisk, or cockatrice, was hatched by a snake from a cock's egg and was part snake, part cock; Shakespeare uses the names interchangeably. They were deadly creatures which killed men by looking at them, and Shakespeare refers to this in *Romeo and Juliet*, where Juliet mentions 'the death-darting eye of cockatrice'. We are told that Coriolanus 'is able to pierce a corslet with his eye'; Volumnia calls herself a 'poor hen', who 'hatched' him and made him what he is. Coriolanus refers to his own fate as a 'trick not worth an egg'.

The play has Coriolanus described twice as a bear – once by his mother, and once by Brutus – which emphasizes his noble, warlike character. The Elizabethans thought that the bear gave birth to its young in an unfinished shape, and by licking them, turned them into bear cubs. This notion probably arose because the afterbirth which covers the newborn cub was observed to be removed by the mother licking it off – which is where we get the expression 'to lick something into shape'. Coriolanus makes complex allusions to this in scene one of Act three, as part of the 'feeding' imagery which recurs throughout the play: he warns that the patricians 'nourish'd disobedience, fed/The ruin of the state', by humouring the plebeians. He urges them to 'pluck out/The multitudinous tongue' before the plebeians can 'lick/The sweet which is their poison'.

Bird references occur many times in *Coriolanus*, and are of two broadly different types: those like the references to crows and doves, which characterize the plebeians as base and cowardly, and those which mention eagles, ospreys and kites, and which emphasize Coriolanus's pre-eminence. The general behaviour of birds was thought by the Elizabethans to be full of omens: the pelican was like Christ, because people said it shed its blood to feed its young; the robin and the wren were charitable birds, which would cover abandoned corpses with flowers, moss and leaves; and it was believed that the swan sang a sad and beautiful song at its death, an idea originating from the Greeks. As with the ancient Egyptians and many civilizations since, the eagle, and birds such as hawks, were thought to be the noblest, because they could gaze at the sun without blinking. In Act two, scene two of *Henry VI* Part three, Richard, Duke of York challenges the Prince of Wales: 'Nay, if thou be that princely eagle's/bird, show thy descent by gazing/'gainst the sun'. In a similar vein, Aufidius fully expects Coriolanus to capture Rome by force of right, as the osprey catches fish, 'by sovereignty of nature'.

Other characters in the play are also referred to with animal comparisons: Volumnia rails against the tribunes as 'cats', in contrast to Coriolanus, who is described twice as a 'tiger'. Cats were the companions of witches, and in *Romeo and Juliet* we meet the adage that cats have nine lives. Some Elizabethans used to hang up cats in leather bottles, and shoot at them with crossbows for amusement. Apparently the cats often survived, and perhaps this is where the adage comes from. Elizabethan ideas of 'fun' were sometimes rather unsophisticated. They put hares on the same level as cats, and Shakespeare uses hares several times as symbols of timidity – as when Aufidius chides Coriolanus to 'Hulloa me like a hare' in the eighth scene of the play, and when Coriolanus berates the plebeians on their first meeting.

Several times in the play horses are mentioned, and usually are used as symbols of military valour, except in Act five when Menenius ironically likens Coriolanus to an 'eight-year-old horse' which has forgotten its mother, just after Coriolanus's great meeting with his mother in scene three. The Elizabethans prized horses highly, and thought that you could endanger your horse's life if you ate an odd number of eggs. It was also thought that horse hairs which fell into a stream would become eels, and the Irish believed that if you ever gave your neighbours fire from your home, your horse would become ill.

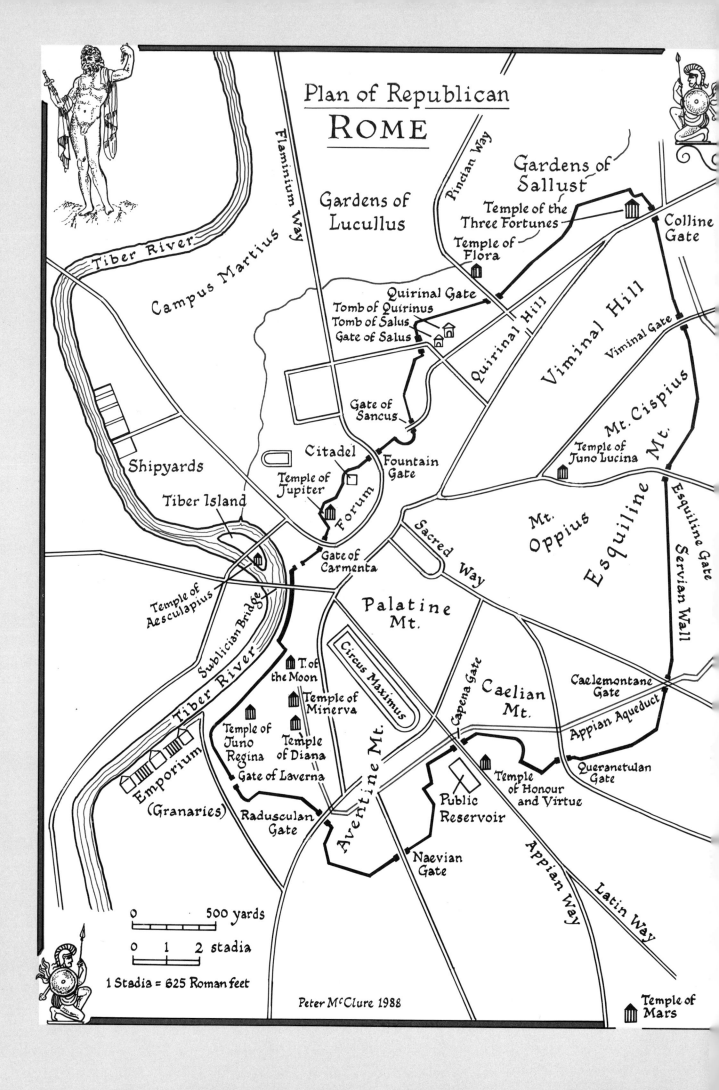

Plan of Republican
ROME

Peter McClure 1988

Tiber River

Flaminium Way

Campus Martius

Gardens of Lucullus

Pincian Way

Gardens of Sallust

Temple of the Three Fortunes

Temple of Flora

Colline Gate

Quirinal Gate

Tomb of Quirinus
Tomb of Salus
Gate of Salus

Quirinal Hill

Viminal Hill

Viminal Gate

Gate of Sancus

Citadel

Fountain Gate

Temple of Jupiter

Forum

Temple of Juno Lucina

Mt. Cispius

Shipyards

Tiber Island

Mt. Oppius

Esquiline Mt.

Esquiline Gate

Servian Wall

Sacred Way

Gate of Carmenta

Temple of Aesculapius

Sublician Bridge

Palatine Mt.

Circus Maximus

Tiber River

T. of the Moon

Temple of Minerva

Aventine Mt.

Capena Gate

Caelian Mt.

Caelemontane Gate

Appian Aqueduct

Temple of Juno Regina

Temple of Diana

Gate of Laverna

Emporium
(Granaries)

Radusculan Gate

Public Reservoir

Temple of Honour and Virtue

Queranetulan Gate

Naevian Gate

Appian Way

Latin Way

0   500 yards

0   1   2 stadia

1 Stadia = 625 Roman feet

Temple of Mars

ETRURIA
AEQUI
Anio
Lake Fucinus
ROMA
Tiberis
Lake Regillus
MARSI
Lake Albanus
Ostia
HERNICI
Sora
Velitræ
Corioli
Cora
Ardea
Norba
VOLSCI
Satricum
Fregellæ
Fabrateria
Antium
Privernum
Liris
MARE ETRUSCUM
VOLSCI
Tarracina
Circeu
Minturnæ
Sinuessa
CAMPANIA
SAMNIUM

LATIUM
Tribal names are underlined

Volturnum
Liternum
Neapolis
Capua
Puteoli

Aenaria

0   10   20 miles

N

The ROMAN FORUM
at the time of
The REPUBLIC

Temple of
Juno Moneta
Citadel
Capitoline
Mount
Fountain
Gate
Senate House
0 200 400 feet
Temple of
Apollo
Temple
of
Jupiter
Capitolinus
Records
Office
Fish market
Sepulcretum
(900 BC)
Temple of
Faith
Tarpeian Rock
Temple of
Saturn
Shops
Sacred
Way
House of
the
Vestals
T. of
Juno
T. of
Piety
Vegetable
Market
Roman Gate
Mugonian
Gate
River Gate
Temple of Fortune
T. of
Aesculapius
Hut of Romulus
Cattle
Market
Tomb of
Hercules
Palatine
Mount
Tomb of
Portunas

1. The Black Stone~
   Grave of Romulus?
2. The Prison
3. Temple of Concord
4. Temple of Venus
5. Temple of Vesta
6. Temple of Castor & Pollux

Understanding Coriolanus
An exploration of the major topics and themes in the play

Summary of themes

It is, of course, Shakespeare's mastery of language that makes him unique, and to appreciate his art fully, a study of the means he uses to make us see and hear what he wanted us to repays the effort.

It has been argued that *Coriolanus* does not follow the pattern of classical tragedy in which a person, usually of high social status, is doomed to disaster and death because of one fatal weakness of character. It is true that in *Coriolanus* the themes of pride and conflict are strong, but there are also complications relating to childhood influences, dissembling speech, and an internecine war between the factions in a body politic. In this tragedy, caste and character are more important than fate.

The major themes and imagery in *Coriolanus* are discussed in detail within the analysis of this guide, and in general in other parts of the introductory sections. Given below is a necessarily truncated discussion which serves to remind the student of issues raised elsewhere in this guide, or to point them in the direction of other areas of exploration.

Body   The earliest and most notable mention of the body imagery in *Coriolanus* is in Act one, where Menenius recounts the fable of the belly. The example serves to illustrate the use to which this metaphor is put throughout the play. It is in the nature of a fable, as William Golding put it, to be 'a story with a human lesson tucked away in it'; and the symbolic nature of the members of the body is well explained in Menenius's tale.

The play uses body imagery in the obvious sense of the physical body and references to it, and also in the sense of the 'body politic' of the Roman State. We can see this parallel usage introduced immediately in the fable of the belly, because the body has no 'head' – the State has no king. The sense of the imagery throughout is that the body is at war with itself, and this even extends to associated imagery – the tongues and mouths of the body are in tumultuous and scathing conflict throughout the play. The voices of the people are raised against the Senate over food shortages, in support of Coriolanus for Consul, attacking Coriolanus as a traitor, and so on. Links to other imagery abound, such as that to sickness when Coriolanus's wounds are dwelt upon – later, he himself becomes a 'wound' to the State as a 'diseased limb'. The citizens talk of putting their tongues into his wounds and speaking for them. Considering the wounding and damage that is caused by intemperate speech in the play, we can see that the metaphor is subtle and complex. No character is immune from the influence of the metaphor – from Volumnia's references to 'the breasts of Hecuba', to Aufidius telling Coriolanus how together they will be 'pouring war into the bowels of ungrateful Rome'; and from what some critics have seen as the overt sexuality of the body imagery, to the final self-destructive image of Coriolanus tearing out his own bowels, and those of his country.

Child   The use of the child as an image in the play begins with the relationship between mother and child when, having been introduced to Coriolanus on the battlefield, we hear the first conversation between his mother and his wife and, shortly after, meet his son. We are invited to compare the son with the father and, by implication, the relationship between the father and the mother. Volumnia and her son have a relationship which many critics have seen as dominated by mother-child considerations; he seems to have identity only within the context of his mother. This is related to ideas about identity and *name*. The second reference to child imagery in this guide is at the point where this other theme emerges from considerations of identity, when Coriolanus cannot remember his benefactor's name. Without a name, the man cannot be identified and saved from slavery. The child-identity-name triangle is present in one form or another throughout the play.

The action of the play is driven by the tensions between Coriolanus's upbringing, his own character and the roles thrust upon him. This results in what amounts to a crisis of identity within the hero and it is often at such points that the child in him emerges, with tantrums of speech and action, culminating in banishment and self destruction – no more so than in the final scene where he holds his mother's hand.

Conflict

The conflict in the play is not confined to the physical acts of insurrection and war, to clubs, raised voices, descriptions of fighting and the symbolic tearing apart of butterflies. The essence of the drama revolves around issues of nations, personalities and things being at war with themselves and this is echoed within the imagery. Notice how, in the play's first scene, there are powerful pairings of contrasting images (see comment 95) which support the contrasting emotions and characters in the play. There are innumerable examples of conflict within the drama, ranging from the obvious to the subtle – notice, for example, how the 'grub' imagery develops through the 'butterfly' to being 'dragon', and how, certainly to some critics, the incoherence of Coriolanus's response to being called 'boy' is a result of an inescapable but irreconcilable internal conflict of personality.

Creatures

These are of two types in the play – the named ones, whose presence is either discussed in the body of the analysis or within the introductory notes, and the less clearly named implicit ones. Of the latter, the most interesting are probably the notions of Coriolanus as a chameleon creature, or of transforming by pupation, and the notion of Coriolanus as a phoenix, attempting to achieve immortality by arising from the ruins of his own destruction.

Disease

Literal examples of disease abound in the play, from the 'scabs' of the populace to the 'diseased limb' which is Coriolanus. Disease in the play is not so much a state of being, as a perception. The imagery of physical disease in the play runs within the context of Elizabethan notions of the causes of health and disease, which are discussed elsewhere in this guide, and which are closely linked with the imagery of conflict. Disease is not depicted simply as a state of ill-health, but also as the tendency to pervert goodness, a disruption of the natural order, as when the life-giving belly is seen as rebelling against the body and seeking to starve it or, worse still, poison it.

Dissembling

The theme of dissembling does not occur simply in the understood context of telling less than the truth, of which there are several obvious examples in the play, but is found in the more powerful notion of being the opposite of assembling. Coriolanus, who is characterized by imagery of hardness and metal, becomes a 'nameless' thing and eventually an automaton and a deity. It is this 'engine' which seems literally to fall apart as the action of the play proceeds. As well as this, the plebeians are tellingly chided by Coriolanus as 'fragments'. This is an interesting allusion, for the plebeians are incomplete, disassembled parts of a whole, of which the rest is represented by other characters in the play – with the notable exception of a 'head' for the enterprise.

The breaking up of things into their component parts is something which we see happening to the Roman State also, and the play is in many ways an exploration of this process of disintegration, which the play seems to suggest is inevitable without the presence of a 'head' for the body politic.

Domination

Much of the time we find that the action in the play seems to stem from the dominant (domineering?) relationship between the mother and the son. The relationship is often explained critically in terms of over-zealous motherly ambition – some form of compensatory behaviour, either for her own unfulfilled personal desires, or as a response to the lack of a father for the boy. The essential issue is one of the abuse of power, which connects the parental issues with those of the larger political and military arenas, and we find considerable discussion in the play of the formal reasons for going to war. Aufidius's disenchantment in Act four serves as a revealing example of how prevalent in the play are incidents bordering on revenge, but driven by bruised pride. We also see the domination of Rome by Coriolanus and of Aufidius by Coriolanus.

Feeding   Frequent mention is made of food, from the corn at the start of the play all the way through to the butchering of Coriolanus at the end of the play. The rioters who open the play are driven by hunger, and it is hunger in one form or another which drives other characters also. An interesting and revealing exercise would be for the student to seek to establish which 'hunger' drives each of the main characters and how they seek to fulfil their need for sustenance. Examples within the text abound, as when Coriolanus warns the patricians against allowing the plebeians to 'feed' upon that [power] which will poison them, and this kind of construction links this imagery to that of a body being poisoned or diseased.

Metal   References to metal or metallic characteristics, such as clashing or clanging, abound in the play, usually in connection with Coriolanus or the mention of him. Coriolanus himself is described as a machine, as are his actions, for example by his mother and by Menenius. The imagery does not, however, simply suggest hardness and inflexibility; the permanence and solidity of personal characteristics and the State of Rome itself is also referred to. The ultimate expression of this is the transformation of humanity into weaponry, as when the soldiers beg Coriolanus: 'Make you a sword of me!'

Payment   References to payment arise within the first few lines of the play, and are only rarely absent thereafter, whether they are as physical as 'crack'd drachmas' and the spoils of battle, or as intangible as the 'dearness' of one's country, the 'debt' one is owed for wounds received, or the 'kindly price' of the Consulship.

   The hero's attitude to 'payment' of any kind sets the tone of the play, for just as he treats battle-spoils as the 'common muck' of the world, so he is unable to value emotional debts and payments, even between mother and son, until the end. The essential dishonesty of doing something for 'payment', rather than for its own sake, is an issue which rouses Coriolanus's passions.

Power   It is the nature and abuse of power which is the central concern of this imagery within the play, underlined by the incident of the butterfly and Coriolanus's son. The proper use of power was a burning issue in Elizabethan times, and Coriolanus's behaviour towards the common people, especially at the time of his asking for voices, would have been of special interest. The corollary of this for the Elizabethans would have been something which we see well demonstrated in *Coriolanus* – the rise of disorder and chaos, and the significance of this for them is discussed elsewhere in the introductory sections of this guide.

Pride   It is the pride of Coriolanus which is identified firstly by the citizens as being something for which he is, perhaps mistakenly, notorious. Evidence exists within the text of the play for arguments that Coriolanus is indeed proud, or that in fact he is actually rather modest, with a possibly over-developed sense of what is 'proper' behaviour for different classes within society. But pride is not something which is exclusive to any one figure in the play, and students will find little difficulty collecting evidence to support a similar charge against most characters.

Service   The notion of service is important for Coriolanus; he begins by averring that service to one's country is worth more than a man's life, and yet he rejects 'payment' for service. Ironically, it is his pursuit of service for its own sake – rewarded by honour – which leads him into what others call treachery. The position is fraught with moral confusion, and becomes increasingly tangled as the action of the play proceeds.

State   The relationship between the individual and the State, as well as the nature of the State itself, form the setting for the surface action of the play against which we see the characters projected. The central importance of this theme is highlighted almost immediately the play opens, by Menenius's little tale to the citizens, and is developed in those terms throughout the rest of the action. Elizabethan notions about the nature of man, the State, and their relationship, are discussed in detail in the introductory comments to this guide.

Stone   Monolithic and architectural imagery is frequently used when characters refer to Coriolanus. The characteristics of the Roman State are frequently described in terms of its physical, architectural features, rather than its spiritual ones, which are the ones that Coriolanus himself usually concentrates on. Imagery of stone, and stone-like things, is frequently found together with that of metal, with its associated overtones of battle and destruction. The action of the play is underpinned in this way, for some of the imagery in the play is threatening to other imagery, as when we find the reassuring solidity of the 'corner-stone of the Capitol' set against several references to the precipitous Tarpeian rock.

Virtue   Whereas Coriolanus has a rigid inflexible code of what is honourable or virtuous, other characters—Menenius and Volumnia being two good examples—rely on a form of situation-ethics for guidance. On the one hand, the rigid approach can be perceived as arrogance or pride, whilst the other approach can be seen as dissembling or opportunism. Several characters in the play suggest that Coriolanus's inability to adopt a more pragmatic approach renders him not only unsuitable for political office—a position we might feel happy to support—but even for citizenship, which is too bitter a pill even for Volumnia.

Voices   There are many 'voices' in the play, from those of the citizens, to those of conscience. Voices are characterized as 'dissembling', 'noble', 'rank-scented' and as reeking 'o'th'rotten fens', depending upon whose they are. We hear voices raised in adulation, in supplication, in anger, in jest and in fear—but rarely in agreement.

The 'voices' imagery connects in a complex way with that of tongues, mouths and feeding, and extends from there into the imagery of food, health and poison. In this sense, the 'begging' of voices by Coriolanus is subtle and apposite, for he is both the military sustenance and the arm of the State, but at the same time his peacetime voice makes him a 'disease', to be removed surgically.

The text of Coriolanus

In 1623 the First Folio (collected edition) of Shakespeare's plays was published by his friends in memory of him—Shakespeare himself had by this time been dead some seven years—and had thirty six plays in it. Before this, some sixteen of the plays had been published as Quarto editions, and for some plays (e.g. *Hamlet*) more than one Quarto exists—they are not all identical. Other Folios were produced in the seventeenth century, but of the plays they contained, only *Pericles* is now thought to be by Shakespeare. *Coriolanus* was not printed within Shakespeare's lifetime.

We think that the First Folio was taken from accurate theatre copies, or possibly even from Shakespeare's own text, because of the nature of the stage directions and some characteristic spellings. However, some of the earlier Quartos have the appearance of 'pirate' copies, which rival theatre companies may have produced from notes made during the performances. The editor of any text therefore has to compare all these sources, attempt to eliminate transcription errors and compositors' errors, and produce a reliable version, although in the case of *Coriolanus* most scholars agree that we have what appears to be a remarkably good Folio to work from. Nicholas Rowe (1674–1718) was the first editor to attempt the production of a reliable text; he also divided most of the plays into acts and scenes, and introduced place references, notes about exits and entrances, and lists of characters.

The First Folio edition of *Coriolanus* has acts marked in it, but no scenes, which were inserted later by Rowe. Even the division into acts may well not be Shakespeare's, as the related work *Antony and Cleopatra*—entered in the Stationers' Register in May, 1608—does not have them. In any case, *Coriolanus* seems to fall into three sections, rather than five: the Volscian war (Rome at war); Marcius's bid for the consulship, and his banishment (Rome at peace); and his return with the Volsces to his surrender and death (dénouement). The Folio does not say where Act five, scene six takes place, although Plutarch sets it in Antium, but as one of the conspirators refers to Aufidius's native town we may suppose that Shakespeare followed his source here, and this is where Rowe set it. Generally speaking, it is as well to ignore details of locale given at the beginning of each scene, as this is almost certainly a feature introduced by Rowe. Where it matters, we can deduce the setting for scenes from what the characters say. The entrances and exits in the Folio are substantially the same as used in modern texts.

The division of acts into scenes would have had no relevance in Shakespeare's day, when the action would have flowed uninterruptedly across the open stage. Rowe probably added scene divisions as a convenience for the theatre of his own time. The end of scenes in Shakespeare is frequently signalled by a character uttering one or more rhyming couplets, although *Coriolanus* is interesting in that it does not use this technique, with the fascinating exception of Aufidius's pseudo-soliloquy in Act four, scene seven:

> One fire drives out one fire; one nail, one nail;
> Rights by rights falter, strengths by strengths do fail.
> Come, let's away. When, Caius, Rome is thine,
> Thou art poors't of all: then shortly art thou mine.

The interesting effect of Shakespeare's virtual abandonment of soliloquy in *Coriolanus* is discussed in more detail elsewhere in this guide.

Shakespeare's output has been divided, notably by Professor Dowden, into several stages. The first stage, of 'dramatic apprenticeship', is generally agreed to be between about 1590 and 1596; next we find the comedies and the English Histories, produced between about 1596 and 1600; then between about 1601 and 1608 the 'grave and bitter comedies' and the great tragedies; and finally between about 1608 and 1612 we have the great romantic plays. All the evidence seems to point to 1608–9 as the date for the writing of *Coriolanus*, which puts it at the end of the stage which Dowden characterizes as 'out of the depths'.

After *Coriolanus*, Shakespeare turned to writing the great romances, which were the last plays he produced. These include such plays as *Cymbeline*, *The Winter's Tale* and *The Tempest*. *Coriolanus* was therefore Shakespeare's last play in which we see explored the relationship between a society and the form of government it exists under. At the time when the play is set, Rome was a newly emergent republic, the wealthy patricians and the common citizenry having together removed the last of a line of tyrant kings, and we therefore see a society in which there is no 'head' in the Elizabethan sense. This must have provided an interesting scenario for Shakespeare, who could not explore such a situation within the bounds of English history, tied up as it was with the notion of the Divine Right of Kings to govern, the notion that the King was God's representative on earth, and a body of law prescribing the manner of each succession. Many of the central issues which arise in *Coriolanus* could not have arisen in other settings where, as happens for example in *Macbeth* and *Hamlet*, the situation is always set within the context of a usurped proper authority, and is finally resolved by the reinstatement of it.

Introduction to the play

Coriolanus was probably written in 1608–9 for production by the King's Men, and was Shakespeare's last tragedy and his last dramatization of Roman history. Like *Julius Caesar* and *Antony and Cleopatra*, *Coriolanus* has often been called a political tragedy; and this may be due to his using Sir Thomas North's translation of Plutarch's *Lives of the Noble Grecians and Romanes* as his source for all three. Plutarch was a Greek who was very interested in political morality, and in *Coriolanus* Shakespeare followed his source extremely closely.

Plutarch (*c.* AD50–*c.* AD120) was a student of Roman history, as well as a biographer and philosopher. He paired off Greek and Roman heroes in his writings, to illustrate his thesis that character is the overriding influence on destiny. Caesar is set against Alexander the Great, for example, and the Athenian soldier Alcibiades is set against Coriolanus. Shakespeare's major alteration to the story of Coriolanus as found in Plutarch is probably in his compression of time, so that for example in the latter it was some time after returning home that Coriolanus stood for Consul, a long time after his failure that he was banished, and even longer still before he finally turned to attack Rome. Similarly, Shakespeare altered certain matters of emphasis – for instance, in Plutarch the common people are much more sensible and have greater political intelligence than do those in Shakespeare's play.

Commentators and audiences alike seem often to have been rather uneasy with Shakespeare's *Coriolanus*, and it appears to have enjoyed relatively little success, at least in an unadapted form, until just before the Second World War. Critics have usually thought of it as a rather inferior tragedy, with no appreciable villain and without the hand of fate spinning the plot; it is argued that *Coriolanus* therefore lacks the essential ingredients of pity and terror. The hero seems shallow and one-dimensional, and we never see a dramatic inner struggle taking place within him. Undoubtedly this is largely due to the almost complete absence of soliloquies, as compared with Shakespeare's other tragedies, but it may also have something to do with a mistaken view of what kind of play *Coriolanus* is. Some critics have held that the perception of the play as a tragedy is erroneous and have argued instead that it should be seen as a purely political play, or as a satire or even as a comedy. Granville-Barker has argued that Shakespeare had just written *Othello, King Lear, Antony and Cleopatra* and *Macbeth* in almost as many years, and perhaps there was some 'ebbing of his imaginative vitality'. On the other hand, T.S. Eliot thought that *Coriolanus* was, with *Antony and Cleopatra*, 'Shakespeare's most assured artistic success'. Some of these views are explored in more detail elsewhere in this guide, but you will need to draw your own conclusions, in the final analysis.

Although Shakespeare's three Roman tragedies, *Julius Caesar, Antony and Cleopatra*, and *Coriolanus*, all have a common source in Plutarch, the argument that they form a natural group relies less on this, or on the fact that they deal with very similar subjects, than on the perception that they adopt the same method of treatment, one which is largely peculiar to them. Each of these plays presents us with a tragic conflict between the State and the individual, set in an historical context. This places them somewhere between Shakespeare's history plays, and his tragedies of character. An interesting view which you should critically assess is that of Simmons, who argues that the integral relationship among these three plays is expressed in their historical pagan environments: 'There are no villains – no Macbeth, Claudius, Iago, Goneril, Regan, or Edmund.' *Coriolanus* is not the only play in which Shakespeare mixed pagan and Christian elements, nor is it the first in which an un-Elizabethan story is written with an Elizabethan tone, but it is the only play he wrote in which there appears not to be a single character who gains our full sympathy and, perhaps significantly, there is not a single character who clowns. Some critics have felt that these elements contribute very considerably towards the play's strikingly even and measured – some would say relentless – tone.

What is also interesting is the similarities which exist among the heroes of *Coriolanus, Macbeth* and *Othello*; they are all soldier heroes, who are placed in situations where their military training cannot help them. They are men of action, whose actions betray their weaknesses as human beings. For Coriolanus, Macbeth and Othello it is this warlike action which defines who they are; they are, to a greater or lesser degree, at a loss outside the world of battle. Notice the contrast with characters like Hamlet and Brutus. For such as these, it is the need for action which they find tormenting. For all three warriors, the most dangerous enemy is found elsewhere than on the battlefield. All three characters discover that they are doomed to destroy themselves, although for each there is the possibility that, through this destruction, they will achieve spiritual wholeness.

Like Macbeth, Coriolanus discovers that the great defender of the State becomes the State's most virulent enemy, but unlike Macbeth, he comes eventually to accept this – he recognizes and renounces his past self, to be born anew; and in his recognition of the truth he is more akin to Othello than Macbeth. In *Othello* the limitations of the hero are explored at the personal level, but in *Coriolanus* they are explored at the level of the State. In *Macbeth* and in *Othello* we find that the central character, for all his self-deception, still has an inner self to expose; it is this inner self with whom we identify and sympathize. In *Coriolanus*, for the most part, we find it hard to identify with and have sympathy for the central character, who seems empty; that is his tragedy. This gives the drama a peculiar feeling of 'distance'. It puts a gulf between the central character and the audience, and makes *Coriolanus* a difficult play to enjoy.

The obvious (but not the only) paradox of *Coriolanus* is that it portrays a man who, it is alleged, is supremely guilty of pride; and this pride is seen as at once both his greatest virtue and his greatest vice. Shakespeare is careful to balance the two opposing impressions very carefully: so much so, that some critics have felt that the play is almost 'mathematical' in its balance, too dispassionate, lacking an essential human warmth; and that this delicate and beautiful balance is actually quite forbidding and bleak. For such critics, the play is a failure; it is a failure because Shakespeare has taken the vehicle of tragedy so deep into an area of moral paradox that we find ourselves immune from its cathartic effect – the drama is beyond the reach of our human pity, and we are therefore beyond the reach of its inhuman terror.

In *Macbeth* there is at the start a feeling that the State is good, and worth preserving – Macbeth's later atrocities are set against the angelic qualities of Duncan and the English King. Considering the fickleness of the plebeians and the deviousness of the tribunes, we might not be able to feel the same way about the Roman State. Again, in contrast to the situation in *Macbeth*, we might read the destructive and divisive behaviour of Coriolanus as echoing that of Hamlet – a symbolic reflection of the discord within the State. Like Hamlet, Coriolanus finds his destructive power turned against enemy and friend alike. In this sense we might argue that Coriolanus becomes an expression of power itself, an inhuman spectre which 'moves like an engine' and 'talks like a knell', and which 'wants nothing of a god but eternity'. If we take this view, he becomes a truly amoral force, and therein lies his terror for others.

In plays like *Hamlet, Othello, King Lear,* and *Macbeth* we find a world in which the powers of good and evil are aligned against each other. Such plays express, in different ways, the same conundrum – that 'fair is foul and foul is fair' – but do so in a context where the audience is usually clear about the greater good and the greater evil. Although the Roman plays also concern themselves with the conflict of extremes, we are less sure about which of them is the extreme of good or evil. The Roman plays create for us a paradoxical world of moral uncertainty. Perhaps in *Coriolanus* this uncertainty persists so strongly because we do not have the insights which are granted to us in plays like *Macbeth* or *Hamlet* by the great soliloquies of their heroes. The student could profitably consider to what extent this is characteristic of all the Roman plays. For example, are there *any* soliloquies in *Coriolanus*, apart from the brief one in Act four, scene four?

Some critics, perhaps sympathizing with the argument above, have suggested that *Coriolanus* is more a dramatized debate than a tragedy. Perhaps the popularity of the play has suffered because it is not a 'literary' play, because the language is less rich in introspection and in soaring vision, because its dramatic force is somewhat obscured until the play is performed. Perhaps *Coriolanus* is, in fact, Shakespeare's most *dramatic* play, in the sense that its energy and power are less evident on the page, but are clear in the theatre.

It may be that the difficulties which seem to arise do so because *Coriolanus*, as Shakespeare's last tragedy, contains aspects which he may have refined and developed from the earlier ones. Perhaps because of this, it is his most sophisticated tragedy, and this makes the play 'difficult'. One reason why difficulty may arise could be because Shakespeare made the imagery of *Coriolanus* subservient to its action; none of the characters is reflective by nature, and we get relatively little sense of their being torn between conflicting passions. As is pointed out in Phillips, Coriolanus himself tends towards the use of simile rather than metaphor, and this gives his language an illustrative, rather than an expressive feel to it – the imagery of the play being less poetic than dramatic in its function. The citizenry, for example, are characterized as 'dogs', 'cats', 'curs', 'hares', 'geese', 'camels', 'mules', 'crows', 'goats' – they are called a 'beast with many heads' and a 'monster'. In contrast, Coriolanus is talked of in terms of a 'dragon', 'eagle', 'tiger', 'bear', and 'osprey' – he is 'the oak not to be windshaken', 'a thing of blood', and 'Hercules'.

In this regard we may see a resemblance to Shakespeare's early work, because in his later plays he moved away from simile towards a much more powerful and complicated use of metaphor. Against this, we can also see far less use of obvious punning than is usually the case in Shakespeare, especially in his earlier work. It could be argued that the starker use of language in the play is in fact perfectly matched to its intention, and that a heavy use of metaphor would have been inappropriate – for is not Coriolanus a 'man of few words'; does he not himself note that 'When blows have made me stay, I fled from words' (2 2 72)? As Shakespeare's most refined tragedy, *Coriolanus* may be an acquired taste. Its sinewy muscularity and dull metallic sheen may make it too ascetic, even acerbic, for most tastes.

As is typical in Shakespeare's work, prose is used for 'base' or comic characters, and poetry for those of higher social status, who lived on a more elevated plane of feeling.

Coriolanus talks in prose to the serving men in Aufidius's house (Act four, scene five), and to the mob. We also see in Act two, scene three, how Coriolanus switches from prose to poetry, depending on whether there are citizens present; it is not only a matter of certain characters always speaking prose or always speaking poetry – intelligence of feeling is being conveyed, as well as social status. Thus critics have noted that the otherwise base first citizen rises to poetry in Act one, scene one, when discussing the fable of the belly, and in Act two, scene one, Menenius and the tribunes speak in prose, as do Volumnia, Virgilia and Valeria, until the entry of Coriolanus, after which they all speak poetry.

The deliberate use of language also extends to the naming of characters in Shakespeare's plays. Books explaining names in the Bible and in classical works were quite common in Shakespeare's day, and Elizabethan and Jacobean writers were often obvious in the way they used them. William Camden's popular *Remaines of a Greater Work* (1605) and revision of *Britannia* (1607) contained glossaries of the meanings of names, and many of his time would have agreed with him that 'names among all nations and tongues . . . are significative, and not vaine senseless sounds'. Modern writers, from James Joyce to Wilson Knight, Nabokov, Harry Levin, Levith and many others, have commented on this aspect of Shakespeare's work. Of course, not all characters in Shakespeare have names with significance – often he was constrained by history, or his sources, for example, but where appropriate, they are touched upon at various points in this guide in the discussion of the text.

The central irony of the play is that it is the honour which Coriolanus seeks which actually dishonours him. This idea recurs again and again throughout the play with, for example, words like 'servant' or 'service' mentioned over twenty-five times. Coriolanus has Hamlet's problem of public duty conflicting with personal moral standards; he also has Lear's problem of being expelled from the world which makes him what he is; like Othello, his rigid moral code can be exploited to his disadvantage; and like Macbeth he becomes (always was?) dehumanized, an expression of the absolute in a world balanced between extremes. The State of Rome has no 'head', and therefore the warrior-servant finds himself thrust into an uncomfortable peacetime role by virtue of his battlefield triumphs. Perhaps, then, the most telling expression of Coriolanus's tragedy is that of Rome itself; that his most ineradicable values – those of the Roman State – serve to eject him from his own world, and ultimately conspire to destroy him. And yet Coriolanus brings no one down with him in his fall. His may be a fall which is accelerated, rather than precipitated, by the actions of others. Could we feel that if the tribunes and Aufidius had not been there, he would have made his tragic errors anyway? True to form, Shakespeare puts the most ironic expression of the tragedy into the mouth of the hero:

> . . . Despising
> For you the city, thus I turn my back.
> There is a world elsewhere!

> (3 3 133–5)

The play opens with a mob who are keen to settle a score with their staves and clubs, and numerous weapons are mentioned throughout the play. The action is littered with references to blood, but always within the context of honour and nobility; the word 'noble' itself is mentioned well over 50 times in the play. This emphasis on blood and on sudden violent injury often appears in a pseudo-sexual context, which is sometimes reminiscent of *Macbeth*:

> . . . The breasts of Hecuba
> When she did suckle Hector, look'd not lovelier
> Than Hector's forehead when it spit forth blood
> At Grecian sword contemning.

> (1 3 40–3)

The State plays a part in the conflict within the Roman plays which we do not see in the non-Roman tragedies. Exiled from Rome, the heroes must eventually confront the city which defines who they are. Rome therefore becomes both the antagonist and the protagonist. In many senses, Rome is a State at odds with itself – the fable of the belly is apposite. Even more so than with Shakespeare's other plays, it would be fatal to try to understand any of the characters outside the context of the play, in this case the almost dehumanized society of Rome. All of Shakespeare's Roman plays seem to create for us a world inimical to love, to friendship and family life; it is a sealed world, inward-looking and harsh. Coriolanus may speak of 'a world elsewhere' but we never see it and nor does anyone else. There is little human interest or romance in *Coriolanus*, and the whole tragedy is presented in terms of the State. In several senses, *Coriolanus* is a tragedy of State, but at the same time the central pivot of the drama is very much more a problem of character than one purely of politics. You will need to decide whether you think the political struggle is merely the background for the tragedy, or an intrinsic part of it.

The style of the play is cold and bare. The imagery, and therefore the world of Rome, is often characterized as hard, architectural, stony or metallic. Both the action and the hero are hedged about with barriers, conventions and obstacles. There is a general sense of constriction throughout the play; men and cities are defined by and imprisoned within their own ramparts. In such an environment, the expression of a mother's love for her son is to be 'pleased to let him seek danger' in the hardness of 'cruel war'. The aristocracy of Rome are the warrior-classes and this implicit caste system is never actually questioned by anyone.

The rather intellectual cast of the play is perhaps well complemented by the full use of dramatic irony which Shakespeare employs. Coriolanus rallies his troops outside Corioli in Act one, scene six:

> . . . If any such be here –
> As it were sin to doubt – that love this painting
> Wherein you see me smear'd; if any fear
> Lesser his person than an ill report;
> If any think brave death outweighs bad life,
> And that his country's dearer than himself;
> Let him alone, or so many so minded,
> Wave thus to express his disposition,
> And follow Martius.
>
> (1 6 67)

Later we are to see how far Coriolanus values his country 'dearer than himself', and we have had hints of this already, as when he goads his retreating soldiers outside Corioli:

> . . . Mend and charge home,
> Or, by the fires of heaven, I'll leave the foe
> And make my wars on you. Look to't.
>
> (1 4 38)

Both Coriolanus and Aufidius have speeches full of dramatic irony, as when Coriolanus is outraged at being called a traitor, and then goes on to become one, or when he learns that Aufidius lives in Antium, and wishes he had 'cause to seek him there,/To oppose his hatred fully'. Similarly, we find Volumnia dedicated to the pursuit of honour above all else, and yet she advocates that Coriolanus should 'dissemble' for reasons of 'policy'. Such reversals and ironies fit well into a play so filled with moral paradoxes.

Analysis chart

Act	Scene	Important events	Places									Aufidius
			Rome	The Capitol	Coriolanus's house	Corioli	The Battlefield	Between Rome & Antium	Antium	Aufidius's house	Volscian Battle-camp	
1	1	Fable of the belly. The Volscians are in arms.	●									●
	2	Volscians realize Rome is forewarned.				●						
	3	Volumnia and Virgilia discuss Martius.			●							
	4	Martius enters Corioli single-handed.					●					
	5	Martius scorns the plunderers.				●						
	6	Corioli falls. Martius pursues Aufidius.					●					
	7					●						
	8	Aufidius and Martius fight. Aufidius escapes.					●					
	9	Martius rejects plunder – is named Coriolanus.					●					
	10	Aufidius vows death to Coriolanus.					●					●
2	1	Coriolanus returns in triumph to Rome.	●									
	2	Coriolanus reluctant to 'show his wounds' for Consulship.		●								
	3	Coriolanus elected Consul – goes to Senate for confirmation.	●									
3	1	Tribunes persuade citizens to revoke Consulship.	●									
	2	Volumnia persuades Coriolanus to 'repent' to the citizens.			●							
	3	Coriolanus banished.	●									
4	1	Coriolanus says farewell to Rome.	●									
	2	Volumnia castigates the Tribunes.	●									
	3							●				
	4	Coriolanus's soliloquy on the road to Antium.							●			
	5	Coriolanus and Aufidius become allies against Rome.								●		●
	6	Panic strikes Rome as they learn of the alliance.	●									
	7	Aufidius reveals his jealousy of Coriolanus to us.									●	●
5	1	Cominius's pleas rejected by Coriolanus.	●									
	2	Menenius is rebuffed by Coriolanus.									●	●
	3	Coriolanus won over by Volumnia. He leaves with Aufidius.									●	●
	4	Menenius and Sicinius learn that Rome is spared.	●									
	5	Volumnia returns in triumph to Rome.	●									
	6	Death of Coriolanus.				●						●

Characters							Themes																	
Citizens	Cominius	Coriolanus	Menenius	Tribunes	Virgilia	Volumnia	Body	Child	Conflict	Creatures	Disease	Dissembling	Domination	Feeding	Metal	Payment	Power	Pride	Service	State	Stone	Virtue	Voices	Page in commentary
●		●	●			●	●		●	●	●	●	●	●	●	●		●	●	●	●	●	●	33
									●											●				37
		●			●	●			●	●		●	●			●						●	●	38
●		●							●	●	●	●										●		39
									●							●						●		40
																●			●	●		●	●	41
									●									●				●		41
●		●						●				●				●		●	●			●	●	41
		●							●			●												42
●		●	●	●	●	●			●		●	●				●		●		●		●	●	43
●		●					●		●			●	●		●	●	●	●	●			●		45
●		●	●				●		●			●				●	●					●	●	48
●	●	●	●	●		●	●		●	●	●			●		●			●	●	●	●	●	50
●		●	●		●	●		●	●		●	●			●	●	●	●	●	●	●	●	●	53
●		●							●	●		●				●		●		●	●	●	●	55
●		●				●		●		●														57
●		●				●			●	●	●	●		●			●	●	●		●	●	●	57
		●							●			●							●	●		●		58
		●						●	●			●					●	●	●	●				58
		●					●		●			●	●	●			●	●					●	59
●		●	●					●	●	●	●	●		●		●	●	●				●		60
		●			●				●	●		●	●	●			●	●				●		61
	●	●	●						●	●				●						●			●	63
		●	●									●			●							●		63
		●	●		●	●	●	●	●	●		●		●	●			●	●	●	●	●	●	64
●		●	●						●	●			●					●	●			●		68
		●	●						●	●														
		●		●				●	●			●	●				●	●	●	●		●	●	69

29

Finding your way around the commentary

Each page of the commentary gives the following information:

1 The act, scene and line number plus a quotation so that you can easily locate the right place in your text.

2 A series of comments, explaining, interpreting, and drawing your attention to important incidents, characters and aspects of the text.

3 For each comment, headings to indicate the important characters, themes, and ideas dealt with in the comment.

4 For each heading, a note of the comment numbers in this guide where the previous or next comment dealing with that heading occurred.

Thus you can use this commentary section in a number of ways.

1 Turn to that part of the commentary dealing with the act you are perhaps revising for a class discussion or essay. Read through the comments in sequence, referring all the time to the text, which you should have open before you. The comments will direct your attention to all the important things of which you should take note.

2 Take a character or topic from the list on page 32. Note the comment number next to it. Turn to that comment in this guide, where you will find the first of a number of comments on your chosen topic. Study it, and the appropriate part of your text to which it will direct you. Note the comment number in this guide where the next comment for your topic occurs and turn to it when you are ready. Thus, you can follow one topic right through your text.

3 A number of relevant relationships between characters and topics exist in the play; many of them are subtle and complex and are discussed in the commentary as appropriate. To get the best out of this guide, you should read the text of the play in conjunction with the commentary but, importantly, in the context of the introductory remarks.

For example, you want to examine in depth the theme of domination in the play. Turning to the single topic list, you will find that this theme first occurs in comment 9. On turning to comment 9 you will discover a zero (0) in the place of the previous reference (because this is the first time that it has occurred) and the number 13 for the next reference. You now turn to comment 13 and find that the previous comment number is 9 (from where you have just been looking) and that the next reference is to comment 15, and so on throughout the text.

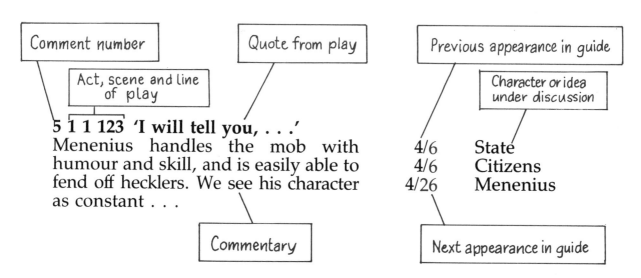

Comment number

Act, scene and line of play

Quote from play

Previous appearance in guide

Character or idea under discussion

5 1 1 123 '*I will tell you, . . .*'
Menenius handles the mob with humour and skill, and is easily able to fend off hecklers. We see his character as constant . . .

4/6   State
4/6   Citizens
4/26   Menenius

Commentary

Next appearance in guide

Single topics:

Characters	Comment no:	Topics	Comment no:
Aufidius	11	Body	3
Citizens	2	Child	13
Cominius	53	Conflict	4
Coriolanus	1	Creatures	7
Menenius	2	Disease	4
Tribunes	26	Dissembling	2
Virgilia	13	Domination	9
Volumnia	1	Feeding	2
		Metal	3
		Payment	1
		Power	15
		Pride	11
		Service	1
		State	3
		Stone	3
		Virtue	1
		Voices	2

It is important to note that the use of references throughout this guide for themes, images, characters or topics is not meant to suggest that such things are not present in parts of the play where they are not mentioned. Only the most important or most telling references have been highlighted and discussed – it would not be possible to identify every image, reference or theme which we can see throughout the play, for the complex interplay of language and action changes these things each time we come to the play. Students should therefore read around the reference, and examine what is said in the light of the text and of the introductory remarks. Remember that the questions which you will find at many places in this guide are there to help you. You cannot be helped if you ignore the questions – try to answer them fully. The comments and questions will frequently point you in contrasting, even contradictory, directions and many of the observations are deliberately provocative in order to encourage you to think for yourself. This is deliberate, for no single interpretation of *Coriolanus* is ever likely to encompass all that the play has to say to us, and it is not intended to suggest that such an interpretation is 'magically' contained within the pages of this guide. In the final analysis it is *your* informed and intelligent response which your teachers, assessors and examiners are looking for.

All act, scene and line references used in this guide are referenced to The Arden Shakespeare edition of the play.

In the interests of greater clarity the play's title-name *Coriolanus* has been used for the central character throughout this guide, irrespective of the given name he may be 'travelling under' at any given moment.

Commentary

Act 1

1 1 1 29 'Consider you what services he has done . . .'

Just thirty or so lines into the play we find the first citizen's answer to this question highlighting the central issue of the drama: what kind of reward, if any, motivates someone to act in a virtuous way? Throughout the play the matter is consistently raised in terms of earthly reward for services rendered. The question is whether the desire for glory is in itself a vice, or whether it is, in effect, a virtue, because of the way it motivates people to perform admirable actions.

Volumnia who, as we see, has trained Coriolanus to pursue honour, has generated this moral confusion: the Roman who is worthy of honour must reject it as a reward, so that honour will surround him even more. It is this attitude towards fame, distinction, and eminence which is the source of the conflict in the play. Volumnia's speech in scene three of this act – 'When yet he was but tender-bodied . . .' – encapsulates the moral complications which run through the drama.

2 1 1 52 'He's one honest enough, . . .'

The citizens characteristically speak well of Menenius, although he often berates them. Even the tribunes seem not to be roused to anger by his uncompromisingly direct attack upon them in the first scene of Act two. You may feel that this is because Menenius is regarded as an old fool and therefore not taken seriously, or because he is respected – perhaps incorrectly – as being non-partisan, or because he is a consummate politician. There is evidence in the text to support several different views of Menenius, who is a more complex and more subtly drawn character than some critics tend to assume. Perhaps you might agree with him when he says 'What I think, I utter, and/spend my malice in my breath.' (2 1 52), although you might feel that this could more sensibly be regarded as a fine piece of rhetoric.

Notice, as you study the play, how Menenius reveals different aspects of his character under different circumstances: to the plebeians he is patriarchal, a wise counsellor and raconteur; to the tribunes he is a scathing critic, skilled only at gibes; to Coriolanus he is a long-suffering father-figure. Menenius, however, does not have an untainted regard for the plebeians, whose 'stinking greasy caps' he noticed were thrown into the air, 'in hooting at/ Coriolanus' exile. . . .' (4 6 132) and whom he characterizes as 'the musty chaff' who are 'smelt/Above the moon.' (5 1 31). This last jibe is an interesting echo of the corn riots which open the play, and an ironic comment on the role of the citizens' voices in the drama. Both references are good examples of Shakespeare's frequent use of imagery to sustain a sense of dramatic unity.

To Coriolanus alone does Menenius remain constant, and you will find evidence in the text which will allow you to regard this either as loyalty to his patrician class, and therefore politically motivated, or as geniune fondness for Coriolanus, and therefore motivated by love.

3 1 1 64 'I tell you, friends, most charitable care . . .'

The play has frequently been called a political tragedy rather than a personal one, and concerns about the body politic and political argument in general do, it is true, carry much of the drama. Barely sixty-five lines into the action, and, significantly, immediately following the introductory comments of the citizens about Coriolanus, the relationship between the individual and the

0/18	Payment
0/19	Service
0/6	Virtue
0/6	Coriolanus
0/13	Volumnia
0/16	Dissembling
0/4	Feeding
0/6	Voices
0/4	Citizens
0/4	Menenius
0/4	Body
0/8	Metal
0/4	State
0/8	Stone

State is outlined to the mob by Menenius. This relationship is to have profound implications for Coriolanus who, like the citizenry, will learn that:

> . . . you may as well
> Strike at the heaven with your staves, as lift them
> Against the Roman state, whose course will on
> The way it takes, . . .

Interestingly, the State in *Coriolanus* seems not to be the idealized one we see in Shakespeare's other plays. The Elizabethan world-order included a vision of the State which was fragile, vulnerable to man's errors of judgement, but cosmic in its dominion. In *Coriolanus* the State, notwithstanding the warning in Menenius's fable, is a thing expressed in imagery of stone and metal. The Roman State is a thing of constancy, and its monolithic and unforgiving qualities give it a relentlessness amounting, at the finish, almost to cruelty.

---

4 1 1 95 'There was a time, . . .'

Menenius recounts the tale of the belly in superb dramatic blank verse, and in so doing expounds in fable the issue around which the entire action of the play pivots. This passage is a key to the whole design and development of the play, and was taken by Shakespeare directly from his sources.

3/8	Body
0/6	Conflict
0/8	Disease
2/16	Feeding
3/5	State
2/5	Citizens
2/5	Menenius

The play opens, significantly, with an argument about the 'corn' and 'grain' which are the food of the 'body' of the Roman State. The contention is that much is being hoarded by the Senate at the expense of the plebeians. As in the action of the play, the literal health and continued existence of the State are under threat. In Menenius's fable, the organs and limbs are in revolt against the body because they mistake the proper function of the belly – seeing what is actually its sacrifice, as mere greed. Although Menenius has in mind the Senate as the equivalent of the belly, the parallel with Coriolanus is that the populace see him as selfish and proud. Just as Coriolanus refuses all reward for his labours, regarding them as reward in themselves, so in the fable the belly acts only in the service of others; and for itself has 'but the bran'.

The fable of the belly sets the keynote of the play for, more so than in almost any of Shakespeare's other plays, the arguing and fighting hardly ever stop, from the play's start to its end. The story itself contains scene after scene of conflict: from street-fighting mobs, through the war with the Volscians, through Coriolanus taking on a city single-handed, to the hero in combat with Aufidius, and to his unsuccessful duel with, and death at the hands of, the citizens themselves. This is important, and shows us something of the Elizabethan view of forms of government other than their own. The Elizabethans commonly held to the three-way classification of governments propounded originally by Aristotle, which was that all governments are essentially either monarchies, aristocracies or democracies. At the time of the play's setting, Rome's government was perceived as a modified form of aristocracy, while Elizabethan England's government was seen as a modified form of monarchy. One form or other of monarchy was the established mode of government throughout Europe in Shakespeare's time; so we can perhaps understand his interest in the curious 'headless' State of ancient Rome. Notice how, significantly, in the fable of the belly there is no mention of the body's head, even though one citizen identifies 'The kingly crown'd head' as something which the belly might propose as its function in reply to the charge of idleness and greed brought against it by the other members.

Later in the play the tribunes call Coriolanus's pride a disease; in terms of the 'belly fable', this is a telling comment, for he is in a sense 'rejected' by Rome's body politic. Coriolanus is an over-pure expression of all that is essentially Roman – his pride has become a disintegrating force, a virulent threat to the life of the State. Eventually, to continue the metaphor of the fable, it is as though the belly were itself to rebel against its detractors, and instead of feeding the body, poison it. This is the theme of the violation of natural order, and the disease imagery which run throughout the play. To Coriolanus, the plebeians are 'scabs'; and to Menenius, Coriolanus is 'a limb that has but a disease'. Significantly, as Spurgeon has pointed out, disease-related images constitute nearly a fifth of all those used in the play, and some have felt – with her – that their repeated use becomes wearisome.

The tribunes were literally officers – originally two, but later ten – elected by the plebeians to protect their interests, whose name was probably derived from *tribus*, meaning tribe.

---

5 1 1 123 'I will tell you, . . .'

Menenius handles the mob with humour and skill, and is easily able to fend off hecklers. We see his character as constant throughout; he is a politician, with the preservation of the State as his first objective. Here he explains the nature of the State to the plebeians, implicitly reinforcing the importance of compromise. His conciliatory skills should not be confused with the attributes of a weak old man – he is an adept politician.

4/6	State
4/6	Citizens
4/26	Menenius

---

6 1 1 166 'He that will give good words to thee, . . .'

Coriolanus makes his first appearance in the play and at once berates the citizenry at length, listing all their faults, in a speech which reveals his physical and moral revulsion at the sight of them. Notice how the opening of the play therefore sets Coriolanus as the only genuinely warlike figure amongst men of peace – the citizens threaten, but never become violent and they retreat quickly once real war appears. We can see the narrowness of Coriolanus's patrician sense of patriotism, disdaining as it does all but his own class.

4/8	Conflict
5/12	State
1/11	Virtue
2/13	Voices
5/16	Citizens
1/8	Coriolanus

Notice also the beginning of a recurrent theme in the play, a preoccupation with 'words', 'voices', 'tongues' and the like, all of which collectively suggest a mistrust of what people say. There are characters like Coriolanus who speak bluntly: 'meal and bran together/He throws without distinction' says Menenius. Contrarily, others who apply more 'policy' to their language – like Menenius himself, for example – argue 'What I think, I utter, and spend my malice in my breath'. The 'voices' of the populace are seen to speak from Coriolanus's wounds, yet be subsequently raised against him because he would not speak kindly when it was politic so to do. Many examples of the questioning of the value of words can be found in the action of the play, and some of the major ones are discussed in the commentary. The constant renaming of Coriolanus is important in this respect also. Volumnia's comment – 'action is eloquence' – is interesting in this context: her son is a man of actions rather than words, and yet he is banished for his words, whilst those for whom eloquence replaces deeds are honoured for what they say, even though it is widely acknowledged that, unlike deeds, the dissembling words of a politician are cheaply bought.

In *Julius Caesar*, Brutus, as a representative of one aspect of the greatness of Rome, is complemented by Caesar; in *Antony and Cleopatra*, we see Antony's greatness both developed and destroyed by his pursuit of love; but in *Coriolanus*, the tragedy is more extreme – for Coriolanus is a personification of the essence of Rome itself. Coriolanus embodies those things which produced both the greatness and the final destruction of Rome – the destiny of both being to rule the world and to destroy themselves. Both Rome and Coriolanus contain within their essential make-up the seeds of their own destruction.

---

7 1 1 171 'Where foxes, geese: you are no surer, no, . . .'
The reference to 'the coal of fire upon the ice' would probably have
reminded Shakespeare's audience of the winter of 1608, when fires were lit
on the frozen surface of the Thames. This and many other contemporary
references give the play a thoroughly Elizabethan setting, and the notional
fact that it is set in Rome, Antium and Corioles around 490 BC would not
have troubled audiences in the 1600s. We find Volumnia mentioning 'the red
pestilence' in 4 1 13, which would have reminded Shakespeare's audience of
the plague epidemic of a few years before, and there are many Elizabethan
figures of speech and names in the play. *Coriolanus* was by no means the first
of Shakespeare's plays to have an Elizabethan setting for a non-Elizabethan
story. We must therefore be careful to recall the context of the drama. Not
least, we should recall that to all intents and purposes it would have been
performed in what was 'modern dress' for its audience.

0/15   Creatures

8 1 1 203 'They are dissolv'd. Hang 'em! . . .'
There is prominent mention of stone and architecture in the play, often in
conjunction with metallic imagery. Here we find Coriolanus referring to the
idea that 'hunger broke stone walls' and later to the city being 'unroof'd' by
the rabble, whom he derides as 'fragments'. Later still, in the sixth scene of
Act four, the impetuous citizenry 'have help to ravish your own daughters,
and/To melt the city leads upon your pates, . . .'.

4/40   Body
6/9   Conflict
4/10   Disease
3/40   Metal
3/53   Stone
6/11   Coriolanus

The atmosphere of constriction and hardness pervades the drama.
Coriolanus particularly is associated with images and metaphors to do with
architecture, most notably in Menenius's 'coign o'th'Capitol' speech in the
fourth scene of Act five. In addition to the emphasis on hard, metallic or
stony imagery, there is continual reference to images of the body, especially
as regards disease, illness and sores. This pervasive 'theming' of the imagery
has on occasion attracted critical comment – not all of it positive.

Some critics feel that Shakespeare's use of imagery in *Coriolanus* is too
evident: they see it as 'overworked', 'very obvious', and 'wearisome', to
quote Spurgeon. Others, however, have argued that the way the imagery is
used forces our attention repeatedly back to the play as a political drama;
and that we therefore have our attention tightly focused throughout on the
argument, rather than on soaring poetry or the human condition. This latter
approach is more usually associated with certain modern playwrights, such
as Bertolt Brecht. You will need to make up your own mind on this by
considering the pros and cons of the argument. Briefly, the allegation is that
the imagery in *Coriolanus* suffers mainly by being obtrusive. Therefore,
whilst one may know *Macbeth, King Lear* or other plays by Shakespeare very
well without necessarily being too aware of the dominating symbolic
structure which underpins the action, it is argued that this is not so in
Coriolanus.

If you feel that this view has some validity, you will need to decide how far
you see the symbols and images in *Coriolanus* as being 'grafted on to' the
action or, instead, as being integral to it. Spurgeon's example, repeated
elsewhere by other critics, is that Coriolanus is referred to as a diseased limb
or gangrened foot mainly because this fits neatly into a preconceived 'body-
disease' theme in the imagery. This is contrasted with Kent's view of Lear's
death in *King Lear*, where the death is seen in terms of the release of a
tortured body from the rack; not because physical torture is a 'theme' in the
play, but because the imagery grows out of the action in an almost essential
way. Shakespeare is rightly admired for the way his imagery and expression
are often indivisible from one another – that is, the content and the
expression are so tightly interdependent that one cannot be divorced from
the other, without completely destroying both. In many places

Shakespeare's work it is impossible even to distinguish between the content and the expression, such was his incredible command of the medium.

In order to make a case that the use of imagery in *Coriolanus* is 'very obvious', you will need to demonstrate by specific example that it frequently does *not* grow organically from the context of the action, but instead jars with that context, in a way which you can demonstrate is rather 'forced'. Critics have argued both ways in the past, and plentiful evidence exists to support either view; the important thing to keep in mind is that you need to be able to offer specific evidence in support of your opinion.

9 1 1 223 'The news is, sir, the Volsces are in arms.'
Rather as is the case in *Romeo and Juliet*, the public issue in *Coriolanus* appears to be a mindless and motiveless conflict. In *Romeo and Juliet* the servants of the Capulets and the Montagues fight because they fight – Tybalt and Mercutio personify man's aggressive and sexual passions at their most unrestrained. In *Coriolanus* the Romans fight because they are attacked by the Volsces, and the Volsces fight because they fight. As in *Romeo and Juliet*, not even a token explanation for this is offered by Shakespeare. Both plays explore some of the consequences of mankind's unending and motiveless struggle to dominate.

8/10   Conflict
0/13   Domination

In *Coriolanus* Shakespeare spends more time than in any of his other plays exploring the formal reasons for going to war. Some critics feel that when Shakespeare wrote his plays he intended that the audience should look behind the action for the causes of events; you may feel that, whether this is the case or not, we justifiably do so. In *Coriolanus* this would mean an attempt to see beyond the public issues to the private ones; and to do this we would look mainly to Volumnia for the origins of the play's action. What evidence could you find to support the view that Coriolanus has been spoilt by his mother? Notice how Volumnia rebukes Virgilia for her weakness towards the end of scene three in this act. Is Volumnia obsessed with her own love of her son's success?

10 1 1 224 'I am glad on't; then we shall . . .'
Coriolanus sees war as something positive and life-enhancing for the State. This view surfaces again in the conversation between the Servingmen in Act four scene five. The image derives from contemporary medical beliefs (see page 12) and hinges upon the word 'vent' as being to do with clearing the sick body (politic) of the superfluous 'humour'. The literary origin of the reference, arising as it does from Plutarch, is well summarized in the relevant footnote in the Arden edition of the play.

9/12   Conflict
8/16   Disease

11 1 1 229 'I sin in envying his nobility; . . .'
This short speech contains one of the most telling pieces of dramatic irony in the play. Caius Martius, talking of Aufidius, says that 'were I anything but what I am,/I would wish me only he.' By being transformed into Coriolanus, he achieves precisely this – he becomes the enemy of the State, the potential destroyer of Rome, the supplanter of Aufidius even in the eyes of the Volscian's own soldiers. A further irony is that, whilst the plebeians of Rome would have flung Coriolanus from the Tarpeian rock, so Aufidius destroys him – both with the cry of 'traitor' upon their lips.

0/20   Pride
6/14   Virtue
0/25   Aufidius
8/13   Coriolanus

12 1 2 11 'The people mutinous; . . .'
Aufidius and Coriolanus understand each other's military situations very well. They use spies and other intelligence to keep themselves informed of the other's troop movements and general state of readiness. Rome in these

10/13   Conflict
6/19   State

days was but one of many city-states, each struggling with the others for territory, conquests and power – hence the need for information. Aufidius is understandably keen to take advantage of any civil unrest, famine or political reverses which come to his notice.

---

13 1 3 1 'I pray you, daughter, sing, . . .'
In this, her first speech, we see Volumnia as a tough and unloving mother, rather Amazonian in her unmaternal attitudes towards her son. She has sought to direct her son in such a way as to gratify her own thirst for honour. She has achieved this, we learn, by withholding love and praise from her son, and is not without a large measure of Machiavellian instinct – as is betrayed by her attitude towards the citizenry in Act three:

0/24	Child
12/18	Conflict
9/15	Domination
6/19	Voices
11/14	Coriolanus
0/14	Virgilia
1/15	Volumnia

> I would dissemble with my nature where
> My fortunes and my friends at stake requir'd
> I should do so in honour. . . .

> (3 2 62)

Do you think that Volumnia always advises her son out of the best possible motives? How far is her affection for him supportive and given openly; how far is it calculated and suffocating? How far is the tragedy of Coriolanus the result of a special kind of parental blindness?

Interestingly, Virgilia takes no part in these manoeuvrings. Does this suggest to you that she has less political expertise, that she is less realistic and is 'softer', that she has a more tender loving nature, or that she exceeds Volumnia in dignity and integrity? You might observe that Virgilia's unobtrusive grace and silence seem to exercise no influence whatever on Coriolanus – or his son, come to that – even, it could be argued, at the end of the play. Although Coriolanus mentions several times his happiness as a bridegroom, husband and father, we find only slight evidence that this affected his ingrained character. What evidence there is largely reveals itself, or does not, in the light of the interpretation you place upon the precise quality of Coriolanus's tragedy in Act five.

It has been argued, mostly by Pitt, that as was the custom in his age, Shakespeare's depiction of women in the Histories confined them to a subservient role. It is suggested that women are of significance only in so far as they illustrate some aspect of the hero's character. This view may be easier to support with regard to Virgilia than Volumnia. Assess who you think is the prime mover in the mother-son relationship. Would you agree that it is Coriolanus who exerts influence upon his mother, or vice versa; or that his behaviour is affected only somewhat by her?

The alliterative quality of the names of female characters in *Coriolanus* – Virgilia, Volumnia, Valeria – suggests a union between them. Shakespeare has used this device also in *A Midsummer Night's Dream*, where we find Hermia, Helena and Hippolyta. The association of the female characters in *Coriolanus* is strengthened by the way they are introduced here, all three together. Consider the extent to which they represent a choric element within the play, or a perceived group within the State acting as a counterpoint to other groups – citizenry, aristocracy, warriors. The forceful Volumnia, a pseudo-'masculine' type, speaks volumes compared with the others; Virgilia's nature is by contrast more reflective and poetic, as befits the association of her name with the Latin poet Virgil. Valeria is an unexplained Latin personal name.

---

14 1 3 38 'His bloody brow? O Jupiter, no blood!'
Only Virgilia seems able to respond to Coriolanus as a human being. To others, he is a hero or a god, but to Virgilia he is always something else. Unlike Volumnia she would not be happy to exchange her husband's life for

11/17	Virtue
13/17	Coriolanus
13/15	Virgilia

a 'good report'. Significantly, Coriolanus always treats his wife gently, although this tender link appears only infrequently in the play, for Virgilia is not often on stage and, when present, is usually characterized by her 'gracious silence'. In this, she symbolizes the human heart of her husband which, in the final analysis, rises triumphant above the hero-god in him.

In his History plays, Shakespeare both did and did not defer to the stereotype his age generally had of women. Indeed, you may agree that all such stereotypes sometimes exist more in popular imagination than in reality. In order to decide how far the subservient, supportive and gentle stereotype of women is prevalent in *Coriolanus*, you need do no more than compare Volumnia and Virgilia, particularly with regard to the extent of their dramatic importance within the play. This is not to suggest that Shakespeare never used stereotypes – witness Calpurnia and Portia in *Julius Caesar*, for example – but that, as a dramatist, he used them for his own creative ends.

---

15 1 3 60 'I saw him run after a gilded butterfly, . . .'
Valeria's description of this brilliantly symbolic incident hints at Coriolanus's attitude towards the weak. The son's behaviour reflects the father's: in the one, we see the other's self-will; in both, the power and the strength are abused.

7/16	Creatures
13/40	Domination
0/40	Power
14/33	Virgilia
13/26	Volumnia

Perhaps understandably, Freudian interpretations of the influence Coriolanus's mother exercises over him abound. The student should be wary of all such attempts to 'understand' the personality of Coriolanus, for he is a *device* used by Shakespeare as a *dramatic vehicle* – he is not a 'real person', and attempts to see him this way will usually pervert our perception of what the drama is all about. That is not to say that we should make no attempt to understand the characters in *Coriolanus* and their dramatic relationship with each other; but we should be clear that we are doing so only within the context of the drama as written. Although it is reasonable to feel that Shakespeare strove to 'hold the mirror up to nature' in his work, and thereby sought to give us insight into nature, it can be dangerous to over-personalize the *dramatis personae* he used.

Valeria's reference to Penelope is as revealing in its reference to Virgilia as is Volumnia's earlier reference to 'the breasts of Hecuba' – both attributions tell us something about the characters to which they attach. During the long absence of her husband Odysseus, Penelope was sought by many persistent suitors, but deflected them with the excuse that she had to finish weaving a robe for her father-in-law Laertes before she could decide. During the night she undid all that she had woven during the day.

Hecuba was the wife of Priam and mother to Hector, Paris and many other children. The Greeks carried her off after the conquest of Troy and used her as a slave. The Amazonian warrior-image of Volumnia contrasts well with that of the image of wifely faithfulness which is appropriate to Virgilia.

---

16 1 4 30 'All the contagion of the south . . .'
Elizabethan folklore had it that diseases came from the south, possibly because of the association of heat with putrescence, or because of the maritime connection with foul-weather winds.

15/47	Creatures
10/26	Disease
2/23	Dissembling
4/48	Feeding
6/21	Citizens

Coriolanus frequently uses images of disease, animals and food in his tirades against others. His normal voice is blunt and critical – notice here how he enters, 'cursing'. As has been alluded to earlier, the use of imagery in *Coriolanus* is largely illustrative rather than poetic. Here, for example, any one of the images could be dispensed with, without affecting the meaning. It is the relentlessness of Coriolanus's abuse which produces the effect here, rather than any specific image or poetic expression. The effect is blunt, spartan and aggressive.

It is important to remember that Coriolanus's attitude to the plebeians cannot be weighed purely in terms of our modern perspective. In ancient Rome – and, come to that, in Elizabethan England – Coriolanus would be seen to be behaving to a considerable extent in the way he was expected to behave. A wealthy aristocrat would be brought up in an environment in which it was implicit that there was a social gulf between himself and the common people. You might therefore feel that Coriolanus is simply a rather immature young man who has yet to learn the political skill of 'dissembling' to the common crowd, as his mother urges him to do. This immaturity might also explain his emotional over-reaction to being called a 'boy' at the end of the play.

___

17 1 4 56 'Thou wast a soldier . . .'

Marcus Porcius Cato (232–147 BC) was a Roman statesman and soldier who made a particularly strong stand against what he saw as the increasing luxury of Roman society. He was elected censor, but pursued his convictions without success, never reviving simpler habits. It is probable that Shakespeare mentions him because he appears in Plutarch:

14/18 Virtue
14/21 Coriolanus

> For he was even such another, as Cato would have a
> souldier and a captaine to be: not only terrible, and
> fierce to laye about him, but to make the enemie
> afeard with the sounde of his voyce, and grimnes of
> his countenaunce.

Compare that passage with the following, parallel passage from *Coriolanus*:

> . . . Thou wast a soldier
> Even to Cato's wish, not fierce and terrible
> Only in strokes, but with thy grim looks and
> The thunder-like percussion of thy sounds
> Thou mad'st thine enemies shake, as if the world
> Were feverous and did tremble.

___

18 1 5 4 'See here these movers, . . .'

This is another example of how closely Shakespeare followed his source, in that Plutarch commonly made mention of drachmas, which were Greek coins of small denomination. The sense of the phrase is nonetheless as clear to us as it would have been to the Elizabethans, a 'crack'd drachma' clearly being of negligible worth.

13/20 Conflict
1/19 Payment
17/19 Virtue

A more contemporary reference can be found in the 'doublets that hangmen would/Bury with those that wore them' – as it was customary in Elizabethan times for the executioner to receive the clothing of those he hanged. The implication here, of course, is that the spoilers are indiscriminate. Bear in mind Cominius's later observation that Coriolanus was outraged: 'Our spoils he kick'd at'. Shakespeare broke with Plutarch here, however. In Plutarch we find that Martius's anger was directed not at the looting itself, but at the unseemly timing of the looting:

> . . . it was no time nowe to look after spoyle, and to
> ronne straggling here and there to enriche them
> selves, whilest the other Consul and their fellowe
> cittizens peradventure were fighting with their
> enemies . . .

Thus Shakespeare adapted his source to ensure that the emphasis was consistent, that Coriolanus accepts no reward for his valour and disdains both the spoils and, by implication, the spoilers, as 'The common muck of the world'.

19 1 6 71 'If any think brave death . . .'
Here Coriolanus speaks of his country as being worth more than a man's life, yet later in the play we see him switch loyalties to Aufidius for 'some trick not worth an egg'. Antium then becomes wife, child and mother to him. He denigrates old friends and would sack the city which gave him birth. Does this show that Coriolanus's moral fibre is weak and prone to break? Is this what happens at the end of the play – does his mother persuade him to see the moral wrongness of his ways? If so, it might appear that his patriotism is no more than self-seeking pride.

18/21	Payment
1/21	Service
12/27	State
18/20	Virtue
13/24	Voices

20 1 8 11 'Wert thou the Hector . . .'
The Romans liked to feel that they were the descendants of the Trojans, who were traditionally hard-working and determined, and who are the 'bragg'd progeny' referred to. Hector was the principal hero in the battle of Troy, where he was slain by Achilles. In historical times, Hector was worshipped.

18/25	Conflict
11/21	Pride
19/22	Virtue

21 1 9 13 'Pray now, no more. . . .'
Notice how Coriolanus instinctively rejects praise, perhaps because he realizes that the giving and receiving of praise is a kind of payment. This may also be because his acceptance of praise from the plebeians would be a kind of acceptance of them, his inferiors. His modesty is therefore perhaps questionable: another form of pride. To decide if Coriolanus is sincere, consider whether he seems irritated by the praise, whether he really believes that others 'Hath overta'en mine act' and whether his wounds really 'smart to hear themselves remember'd'.

19/22	Payment
20/23	Pride
19/36	Service
16/24	Citizens
17/23	Coriolanus

22 1 9 39 'And stand upon my common part . . .'
Coriolanus refuses the offered one-tenth part of the spoils and says he will settle for the same as the other combatants. You may argue that this shows his personal disregard for wealth, which makes him generous, or that it reveals the stubbornness of his pride, which makes him mannered.

21/31	Payment
20/23	Virtue

23 1 9 64 'Martius Caius Coriolanus!'
Cominius awards Coriolanus his name. Throughout the play we see Coriolanus given several new names, each one increasingly distant in its associated role from his original name. Martius seems to be the only name he is ever given which accurately reflects his character; the other names seem to call upon Coriolanus to perform ever more impossible parts in the drama. In this context, it is interesting to note how frequently Coriolanus comes to refer – always disparagingly – to 'acting' different parts. His fame has brought him these different roles, but his character is unsuited to dissembling – unless, of course, we see him as a character who, right until the end, is deceiving himself.

16/25	Dissembling
21/24	Pride
22/32	Virtue
21/24	Coriolanus

Note that here, rather confusingly, there is conflicting evidence as to whether or not Coriolanus is proud, in the way in which he reacts to the adulation which accompanies his new name: 'I will go wash'. This may be taken, together with his several admonishments to others not to praise him, as evidence of genuine modesty. Alternatively it may be taken, together with his attitude to the citizenry, as evidence of consummate arrogance.

---

24 1 9 80 'I sometime lay here in Corioles, . . .'

Shakespeare seems to have manufactured an incident here to show that Coriolanus does not hate the citizenry as a class of people, but only their well-meaning laziness, stupidity, greed and fickleness. The only gift he begs after his victory at Corioles is freedom for a poor man who looked after him. However, critics who feel that Coriolanus's behaviour always arises from his pomposity and pride, rather than from the true workings of his heart, will point to the irony in the fact that Coriolanus cannot remember the poor man's name. This is a particularly interesting touch by Shakespeare, given the preoccupation with Caius Martius's names throughout the play, and the fact that he himself has only just been dubbed 'Coriolanus'. Names are, for Coriolanus, unimportant, but it is interesting to note that without a name the old man can receive no 'voices', and therefore no mercy. At the end of the play Coriolanus is stripped of his name also, and similarly receives no mercy thereafter.

The strong association between identity and name for Coriolanus is poignant. Just as he cannot remember his host's name, so, as the play develops, he assumes different names, until at the end of the play Volumnia accuses him of being unable to remember his own humanity. He has forgotten who he is – 'As if a man were author of himself/And knew no other kin'.

13/55	Child
23/26	Pride
19/31	Voices
21/29	Citizens
23/25	Coriolanus

---

25 1 10 24 '. . . My hate to Martius. Where I find him, . . .'

Aufidius vows that wherever he finds Coriolanus, he will 'wash my fierce hand in's heart'. This scene contains a powerful irony, for whilst Aufidius swears vengeance, even if he find Coriolanus 'at home, upon my brother's guard' (that is, enjoying his brother's protection); and yet later, in Act four, scene five, Aufidius welcomes Coriolanus rapturously into his house. As Aufidius's first Servingman pointedly remarks, 'Here's a strange alteration!'

The other parallel we can see here is that between the present fate of Aufidius, cast out from the city of Corioles, and Coriolanus, who will be cast out from Rome.

20/27	Conflict
23/32	Dissembling
11/71	Aufidius
24/33	Coriolanus

Characters and ideas
previous/next comment

Act 2

26 2 1 34 'I know you can do very little alone, . . .'

Menenius castigates the tribunes for criticizing Coriolanus, for they are as proud as he. There is a destructive triangle within the play, and at each apex we find pride: first, there is the pride of Coriolanus and his mother, secondly there is the pride of Aufidius, and thirdly the pride of the tribunes. Coriolanus ricochets between the three, being finally destroyed by the way the triangle creates antagonisms at every turn. This self-generating and self-destroying pride is frequently characterized by metaphors of disease, which occur throughout the play.

Although few characters emerge unblemished, you may feel that it is the tribunes who are the real villains of the play. Menenius could be said to be hypocritical in his attitudes towards both Coriolanus and the tribunes, for he castigates them by turn. Volumnia remains hard to the last, seemingly indifferent to her son's tortured situation and blind to her part in putting him there. Coriolanus himself is drawn in a rather cold and detached way by Shakespeare.

27 2 1 37 'You talk of pride. O that you could . . .'

Menenius is an able orator, whose speeches are filled with pointed humour. He seems able to deflate the citizenry and tribunes alike, without arousing anger. The abuse which Menenius and the tribunes fling at each other in this scene is characteristic of their attitudes towards each other, and points up the strong political tensions and divisions which run through Roman society.

Johnson felt that the 'eyes' reference here related to the fable in which a man has two bags around his neck – one before, and one behind. Into the one before him he put his neighbours' faults, and into the one behind, his own. Thus men always have their neighbours' faults before them, but never see their own. However, appealing though this is, it is doubtful if it is the correct allusion, for the sense of the passage is that the tribunes are to turn their vision inwards. As Brockbank notes in the Arden edition of the play, we should compare the suggestion here with the line in *Hamlet*: 'Thou turns't my eyes into my very soul'.

28 2 1 46 'I am known to be a humorous patrician, . . .'

Menenius does not take himself too seriously, and this self-description is apt. Throughout the play we see him pouring oil on troubled waters, although on several occasions he offers partisan opinions. You will need to judge, for example, whether he is always the true friend of Coriolanus. 'Humorous' may have been intended as a pun on 'humour', meaning disposition or inclination, to imply chameleon-like behaviour on Menenius's part.

Sometimes Menenius sides against the tribunes; for example, he says to Volumnia in scene two of Act four: 'by my troth, you have cause', after she has berated them. He also regards Coriolanus's rage at them as 'worthy' in scene one of Act three – although in the same scene, the politician in him recognizes that the people's outrage at Coriolanus 'must be patch'd with cloth of any colour', and we find him addressing the tribunes as 'worthy' and confirming to them that Coriolanus is 'a limb that has but a disease'. Then again in scene two of Act three we find Menenius siding with Coriolanus against the mob:

Characters and ideas
previous/next comment

16/28	Disease
24/30	Pride
5/27	Menenius
0/27	Tribunes
15/30	Volumnia
25/37	Conflict
19/46	State
26/28	Menenius
26/28	Tribunes
26/30	Disease
27/30	Menenius
27/29	Tribunes

Before he should thus stoop to th'herd, but that
The violent fit o'th'time craves it as physic
For the whole state, I would put mine armour on,
Which I can scarcely bear.

You may not feel able to accept Menenius's estimation of his own character –
'What I think I utter' – and may think instead that his comment after
Coriolanus's banishment more aptly sums up his attitude: 'All's well, and
might have been much better if/He could have temporiz'd'. He seems to
have a kind heart, and is moved to tears as Coriolanus leaves Rome in
banishment in Act four scene one: 'Come, let's not weep.'

Menenius acts as a humorous and even-handed commentator, who tries
throughout to exert a moderating influence on the action. An echo of the
disease imagery occurs just prior to the exit of Menenius in this scene, when
he makes the telling remark that the conversation of the two tribunes would
'infect' his brain if he listened to any more of it. The notion that the citizenry
are not intrinsically antagonistic to Coriolanus is highlighted when
Menenius's parting shot draws attention to the role the tribunes are playing
in the drama: he calls them 'the herdsmen of the beastly plebeians'.

---

29 2 1 54 '. . . wealsmen as you are – I cannot call . . .'

Lycurgus was a semi-mythical figure, credited with remodelling the Spartan
constitution to eradicate anarchy and licentiousness. Menenius is being
cutting: the tribunes, being men of the common weal, are riddled with the
commoner's anarchic and fickle temperament. As he goes on to say, he finds
that what they say reveals 'the ass in compound with the major part of your
syllables'.

24/38	Citizens
28/44	Tribunes

---

30 2 1 89 'Yet you must be saying Martius is proud: . . .'

The time 'since Deucalion' refers to the time since the flood, as in Greek
mythology, Deucalion and his wife Pyrrha were the sole survivors who
repopulated Earth. Menenius's speech is full of classical references, as is
much of the rest of the play – a few lines further on he throws his cap to
heaven with the words 'Take my cap, Jupiter, . . .'. As with Lartius's
mention of Cato at the end of scene four of Act one these are anachronisms,
as is Menenius's mention of Galen, a famous Greek physician, a few lines
further on – although given the numerous references in the play to disease,
humours and health, the latter inclusion is perhaps appropriate.

28/49	Disease
26/34	Pride
28/46	Menenius
26/32	Volumnia

Volumnia's reference to Tarquin at line 149 may be more telling. North's
Plutarch has it that Tarquin

had bene king of ROME, and was driven out for his
pride, after many attemptes made by sundrie battells
to come in againe, wherein he was ever overcome.

Tarquin returned to attack Rome once more and afterwards honoured
Coriolanus with an oaken garland because of his valour in the battle. But
Tarquin and Coriolanus were on opposite sides and there is an interesting
parallel here between Coriolanus and Aufidius.

---

31 2 1 150 'One i'th'neck, and two i'th'thigh – . . .'

Menenius and Volumnia total up the wounds of Coriolanus as though they
were votes. This notion is made explicit in the imagery used by the citizens
in the third scene of this act, where they say they will 'put our tongues' into
the wounds of Coriolanus so that the wounds may 'speak for them'.

22/35	Payment
24/42	Voices

32 2 1 157 'These are the ushers of Martius: . . .'
Volumnia describes her son in terms of a Colossus or a god; as 'Death, that dark spirit'. It is her vision which moulds him to what he is, for it is his mother who persuades him to go to the forum, then to apologize to the plebs, then to go back on his word to Aufidius. Although Coriolanus's end is partly a result of his own hot-headed tactlessness, you should consider to what extent it is also engineered by his mother.

25/35	Dissembling
23/34	Virtue
30/46	Volumnia

33 2 1 170 'Nay, my good soldier, up; . . .'
The kneeling of Coriolanus to his mother is parallelled later by her kneeling to him. The irony is in the differing contexts, although in a sense both occasions are triumphant for Coriolanus.

Interestingly it is some time before Coriolanus notices his wife, and has to be reminded by his mother of her presence. Consider to what extent the honorific 'gracious silence' is unintentionally ironic.

25/38	Coriolanus
15/56	Virgilia

34 2 1 201 'I had rather be their servant in my way . . .'
Coriolanus seems well aware of his own limitations and his own character. Unlike almost everyone else around him, Coriolanus does not expect of himself anything which is not intrinsic to his nature. The text abounds with references to Coriolanus's unchanging nature: even one of the citizens who opens the play – ironically calling, not for the last time, for Coriolanus's death – notes that pride is something which 'he cannot help in his nature'.

30/40	Pride
32/36	Virtue

35 2 2 5 'That's a brave fellow; but he's vengeance . . .'
The two officers act as a choric element in this part of the play and, as we would expect, their analysis of the situation is balanced and considerably more impartial than much of the rest of the comment in the play. Notice how it is explicitly acknowledged that politicians lie and dissemble to the common citizenry, in order to gain 'voices'.

32/39	Dissembling
31/36	Payment

36 2 2 75 'I had rather have one scratch my head . . .'
Coriolanus is indeed constant in his rejection of accolades. Here there is a double irony. Coriolanus leaves just as Cominius launches into a 'monstering' of his deeds in a forty-one line speech, the imagery of which ranges from calling him 'Amazonian' (an interesting reference in itself, given the powerful influence over him of his mother), to alluding to him as a powerful 'sea', summoning 'death's stamp' and striking cities 'like a planet'. The second irony is dramatic in that it lies in the future, for Coriolanus will indeed 'monster' his own deeds; he will become a 'dragon', something 'made by some other deity than nature' which 'moves like an engine' – he will become a traitor to all who knew him.

35/41	Payment
21/41	Service
34/37	Virtue

37 2 2 82 'I shall lack voice: the deeds of Coriolanus . . .'
The Elizabethan audience would not have regarded the deeds of Coriolanus as mere dramatist's hyperbole, for there is a sense in which he is more a portrait of an Elizabethan military adventurer than a Roman soldier. Popular Elizabethan history was filled with tales of individual bravery in battle, and Shakespeare may well have been exploiting this resemblance. As Jorgensen, for example, has pointed out, Essex, a brilliant fighter but poor general, habitually led charges, rather than directed them, and an Elizabethan audience would have been unlikely to have missed the parallels:

27/39	Conflict
36/38	Virtue

My Lord of Essex was one of the first that got over
the walls, followed by the souldiers as the place
would give them leave.

                                  (*The Commentaries of Sir Francis Vere*)

---

38 2 2 83 'It is held/That valour is . . .'
Coriolanus has much valour, and hence much virtue. If Coriolanus feels that
the mob have no valour then perhaps we can see why he holds them in such
contempt and why he is angered by any suggestion that they should judge
him. The subtle irony of this can best be appreciated by referring to a
passage in Plutarch's *Life of Caius Martius Coriolanus*:

> Now in those dayes, valiantnes was honoured in Rome
> aboue all other vertues: which they call VIRTUS, by
> the name of vertue it selfe, as including in that
> generall name, all other speciall vertues besides. So
> that VIRTUS in the Latin, was as much as
> valiantnesse.

The irony lies in the assertion that Roman valour encompasses all other
virtues, for in Coriolanus we see valour as wholly *exclusive* of other virtuous
traits.

37/40	Virtue
29/43	Citizens
33/42	Coriolanus

---

39 2 2 96 'When he might act the woman . . .'
The main subject matter of *Coriolanus* is usually taken to be politics and war.
But some critics, notably Berry, have found a strong vein of sexual imagery
in the play – note, for example, the ambiguous verb 'act' in the quotation
above. Supporters of this view tend to see war and sex as the underlying
themes of the play, and you should consider the evidence carefully before
reaching your own conclusion. Think, for example, of all the metaphors of
'acting' used by Coriolanus, or used about him, and see how a sexual
interpretation of the word adds to, or detracts from, the insight into human
nature revealed in the drama.

37/40	Conflict
35/41	Dissembling

---

40 2 2 100 'And in the brunt of seventeen battles . . .'
In this important passage we find Coriolanus surrounded by a swirl of
telling imagery; we have him 'driving', 'bestriding', 'brow-bound with the
oak'; we find that his 'every motion was tim'd with dying cries' and that he
'struck Corioles like a planet'. This 'thing of blood', its sword 'death's
stamp', whose attention is 'pierced' by the 'din of war', is 'reeking' (smoking
with blood) 'o'er the lives of men'.

This terrifying description conjures up man as the personification of a
weapon, charging through the action of the play. He is iron, he is blood, he
is death. Towards the end of the play the transformation is complete; he
becomes relentless, mindless, a machine:

> . . . he no more remembers his
> mother now than an eight-year-old horse. The tart-
> ness of his face sours ripe grapes. When he walks, he
> moves like an engine and the ground shrinks before
> his treading. He is able to pierce a corslet with his
> eye, talks like a knell, and his hum is a battery.

                                              (5 4 16)

Within the honour and pride which form the terms of his own reference, he
has become perfection. Like a thing of perfection, he pursues his wars not
for his own sake, nor for the sake of Rome: they are their own justification.

8/43	Body
39/41	Conflict
15/74	Domination
8/56	Metal
15/45	Power
34/55	Pride
38/41	Virtue

Throughout the play, Coriolanus follows his path 'like a planet', blindly whirling through the dark.

But there is a sense in which this mechanistic emphasis is not the whole story. Also present are the face, foot, chin, spirit and flesh of a man – 'a thing of blood'; we have references to 'acting the woman'; to 'bristled lips'; we see him swinging and lurching as others 'fell below his stem'; and everywhere we hear cries and panting. Several critics have pointed to this implicit sexuality; the scene abounds with Elizabethan bawdy – Tarquin (who was a rapist) is said to 'make a head', we have references to 'bestriding', 'stamp', 'press', 'mark' and 'strike'. The idea is of being 'man-ent'red' by something which 'waxed like a sea', 'whose every motion was tim'd with dying cries', and which 'enter'd the city's mortal gate'. The equation is of virility with a ship's prow, a sword and a metal die. The suggestion is that this is somehow a combat in virility, that war is somehow an equivalent of brutal rape, a kind of ugly predatory lust.

A further insight into the sexual roots of the warrior-code of Rome can be gained by looking in the light of the above interpretation at the meeting of Aufidius and Coriolanus in scene five of Act four, where Aufidius seeks to 'twine/ Mine arms about that body', and where his emotions run to consummation:

> . . . more dances my rapt heart
> Than when I first my wedded mistress saw
> Bestride my threshold.

---

41 2 2 124 'Our spoils he kick'd at, . . .'
As in Plutarch, Coriolanus disdains the Volscian spoils, regarding both them and the reward of fame as tainted – 'a bribe to pay my sword', as he puts it in the early part of Act one, scene nine. For Coriolanus, virtue itself is its own reward.

Is this the dilemma faced by the soldier who is conscious of his own integrity? Can Coriolanus acknowledge his own virtue without destroying it? Conversely, can we sensibly expect Coriolanus to be blind to the virtue in his own military achievements? Do you sense that Coriolanus is aware of his own virtue and, if so, does this transform his actions into something other than virtue?

Can you accept that it is possible for a noble act to be committed by someone who is conscious of the nobility of the action *as he does it*? Or can a noble (or brave, or virtuous) action only be committed by a person who acts *without* consciously thinking about what he is doing at the time? Whichever conclusion you come to, see if you are consistent and arrive at the same view when considering people's wrong or evil actions – that is, do you believe that a person can *only* commit an evil or wrongful action if he perceives it to be so?

The paradox is complete, and Coriolanus's moral situation is, of course, quite hopeless. If Coriolanus accepts anything – even the 'good report' of others 'in token' of his deeds, which Cominius speaks of in Act one, scene nine – then he has effectively accepted a payment for virtue. This would undermine the purity of his motives and therefore of his virtue. Some critics have argued persuasively that Coriolanus compromises his sense of honour at the point where he accepts the name 'Coriolanus', for this too is a kind of payment.

40/46	Conflict
39/42	Dissembling
36/42	Payment
36/55	Service
40/43	Virtue

42 2 3 1 'Once, if he do require our voices, . . .'
Many critics have argued, probably rightly, that this scene challenges the
sympathies and judgement of the audience more than any other in
Shakespeare. Most critics have judged Coriolanus's behaviour here to be
wholly reprehensible, but the student should weigh all sides most carefully.
Given what we already know of Coriolanus, it seems impossible that he
could emerge with his character unscathed from this ordeal, but in fairness
to him it is difficult to see how this would be different for *any* of
Shakespeare's noble figures.

It is not difficult to side with the majority of the critics in condemning
Coriolanus. If you too feel only slight sympathy for him, reassess your
judgement after considering the fact that he is forced against his will into an
impossible situation: should he jettison his integrity? The citizens say that
the price of the consulship is 'to ask it kindly'; in that 'kindly'; is a world of
meaning. Coriolanus, as a member of the patrician class, was expected to
behave according to his 'kind' in publicly acknowledging the human dignity
of the citizenry, even if he did not truly mean it. The citizenry had come to
expect this sort of dissembling, in any case. Coriolanus's action would also
be 'kindly' in both senses of 'considerate', for throughout the play there is
ample acknowledgement from the plebeians that Coriolanus is deserving of
honour.

---

43 2 3 5 'For, if he/ show us his wounds . . .'
Here, the third citizen argues that Coriolanus's 'noble deeds' must produce
their 'noble acceptance' of them. A prospective consul had to show that he
cared for the community, was at one with them and was prepared to
sacrifice himself for them. Coriolanus's refusal to show his wounds is
therefore a rejection of these marks of his humanity, a refusal to reveal the
ordinary man who received them. Although the plebeians may act like
beasts, they are, like Coriolanus, human beings – as Brutus observes to him
at the beginning of Act three:

> You speak o'th'people
> As if you were a god to punish, not
> A man of their infirmity.

> (3 1 79)

The behaviour of Coriolanus at this point could therefore be interpreted as
his refusal to accept his own common humanity, which is the bond between
him and the plebeians. He cannot accept that those very qualities which he
despises in them must also be integral to his own character. In this we may
feel that Coriolanus is more than a little unfair to the citizenry. For although
the plebeians are simple, fickle and easily swayed by the tribunes later on,
they are also generous in their simplicity – they recognize the greatness in
Coriolanus. The plebeians feel that Coriolanus has a right to be honoured,
and therefore the price of the consulship is merely 'to ask it kindly'; and
when he cannot manage even that, they give it to him anyway.

The citizens say they will recognize the precise extent of Coriolanus's
sacrifice: they are to put their 'tongues into those wounds and speak for
them'. Because they accept Coriolanus's sacrifice, the citizens are made
noble. This acceptance is an echo of the Christian acceptance of Christ's
sacrifice. The parallel being drawn is that by accepting Coriolanus's sacrifice,
the citizens are participating in its benefits. Should Coriolanus therefore
accept their voices, he would not so much be accepting what is his 'due', as
what is offered in mutual recognition of nobility. That the imagery appears
more grotesque than religious may be due to its appearing in a pagan
setting.

---

*Characters and ideas
previous/next comment*

41/44	Dissembling
41/43	Payment
31/46	Voices
38/44	Coriolanus

40/50	Body
42/62	Payment
41/45	Virtue
38/46	Citizens

44 2 3 140 'Is this done?'
Coriolanus is evidently relieved that the ordeal is over, for now he can cast off his 'wolvish toge' and change back to 'knowing myself again'. The comment by Menenius that Coriolanus has stood his 'limitation' is double-edged, for he has indeed gone as far as he can in dissembling and has demonstrated his limitations. The tribunes are immediately critical of Coriolanus's apparent success. Does this suggest to you that they are determined that he shall fail, and does their subsequent behaviour bear this out?

42/45	Dissembling
42/46	Coriolanus
29/45	Tribunes

45 2 3 227 'Say you chose him . . .'
Some critics see this last piece of advice by the tribunes to the citizens as being a cowardly attempt by them to keep in with both sides. On the other hand, we may feel that the tribunes are simply giving the people a protective excuse to allow them to revoke an over-hasty and unwise decision. If we grant the tribunes some integrity, we may conclude that they are desperate men who know that the citizens will revolt against Coriolanus when they know his true nature, and they are therefore simply trying to head off a catastrophe. Do you feel that the tribunes are honest men, or are they self-serving rogues?

44/55	Dissembling
40/46	Power
43/49	Virtue
44/50	Tribunes

Act 3

46 3 1 22 'The tongues o'th'common mouth. . . .'
Interestingly, Coriolanus seems to have no hate for the Volsces – indeed, he seems rather to like them as necessary sparring partners. Instead, his hatred is directed wholly towards the Roman plebeians, who throw up questions, problems and demands which he finds difficult to resolve by his warrior-code of combat.

You should carefully consider the extent to which Coriolanus's rage is something of an automatic reflex, like a jack-in-the-box. If this is true, it makes Coriolanus's anger and pride seem rather artificial and shallow. Your feelings about this may also colour your view of the extent to which Coriolanus is actually his mother's puppet. For example, notice the difference between his arrogant(?) attitude towards other people in the play and his attitude towards his mother, which is pointedly summarized in Phillips as 'infantile cowering before his mother's severity'. Does his repeated quailing before his mother deprive Coriolanus of the dignity necessary for a character to become a tragic hero? Critics who sympathize with this view are understandably inclined to see the play as a satire.

Some critics have noted that Shakespeare's *Coriolanus* is far from being a conventional tragedy; it is difficult ever to sympathize with the central figure, and the plot is filled not with a spirit of tragedy, but with a spirit of derision at every turn. The play has been dubbed a satire by some because of this. A. C. Bradley felt that the play was a failure as a tragedy, because Shakespeare follows his source too closely, and 'takes the line of least resistance' in this respect. Another critic, Bernard Shaw, may have hit upon more of the truth than he is sometimes credited with when he observed that the play is not a tragedy at all: his succinct, if whimsical, summary was that 'it is the greatest of Shakespeare's comedies'.

You will need to consider all sides on this, the most difficult of things: the supposed *intentions* of the drama. The issue revolves around a basic difference of opinion about Shakespeare's writing, which raged for many years – whether we should see the plays in terms of its author's intentions, whatever they may have been, or whether we should see them in terms of their universal appeal, but set against the context of their time. As far as establishing Shakespeare's personal intentions, opinions or views is concerned, a search of his writings – especially his plays – seems doomed to certain failure. Some critics have held that in *Coriolanus*, Shakespeare was simply expressing the commonly held view of his age, that putting power into the hands of the citizenry would produce disaster. If this is the case, then in this Shakespeare was at one with all political theorists of his time. Contrarily, other critics have remarked that Coriolanus's behaviour is an exposé of the brutal tactics which all dictators have to adopt in order to retain power, You could argue that there are some elements of truth in both views, but you will have to decide for yourself which interpretation you favour most. The important thing is to be clear about your own views and to be able to offer evidence *from the play*, both to support your own conclusions and to refute those of others.

The general structure of *Coriolanus* does seem different to the pattern Shakespeare adopted in his other tragedies. Shakespeare's tragic heroes usually have very pronounced noble characteristics, which appear at various times during the play. We, the audience, therefore see them torn between the forces of goodness and evil, or order and disorder. Usually we have characters who praise the hero at the start of the play, either for what he is or for what he once was. Then we have soliloquies, spoken by the hero, which reveal to us his inner struggles with good and evil, and which engage our sympathy for him. Just as the hero reaches the very brink of disaster, we usually find that Shakespeare makes him speak words which recall him to us as he was before fate snared him. After the death of the tragic hero there is usually a scene where a character summarizes the hero's fall from grace and ultimate fate. Very little of this happens in *Coriolanus*, where the hero is almost universally denigrated from the outset.

Throughout the play, people make comments about Coriolanus: citizens, tribunes, servants, officers putting out cushions in the Capitol, ladies of the household, travellers on the road; all are constantly talking about Coriolanus. You will find it difficult to come upon one of these references which is not hostile to Coriolanus. Even his mother's attitude is a kind of hostility: a rejection of a loving human relationship. Perhaps Menenius is, on balance, favourably disposed towards the hero, although even so you may feel, along with some critics, that Menenius, as the 'fool' character in the play, is expertly designed to deflate and mock both tribunes and hero alike, and therefore his knowing jibes provoke our sympathy as well as our laughter.

---

47 3 1 32 'Are these your herd? . . .'
Coriolanus again berates the citizenry, this time for their fickleness, for the way they can support something and yet 'straight disclaim their tongues'. He argues that the mob are unable to take a consistent or balanced view of things, and he feels that they are easily led. The impression is given that the mob would be easily fooled, and helpless without a leader. They are good only at shouting, as when Coriolanus returns from Corioli; when he is given their voices for consul; and when he is rejected and eventually killed.

46/48	Conflict
16/61	Creatures
46/48	Voices
46/49	Citizens
46/49	Coriolanus

---

48 3 1 36 'Be calm, be calm.'
To his credit, Menenius strives mightily to deflect the rising tide of 'unbolted language' on both sides. Clearly Coriolanus cannot see that the tribunes are goading him for their own purposes, or if he can, he does not care; but do you think that Menenius can see this? What are the motives of Menenius here? Notice the references to corn again – this is a recurring topic in the play and echoes both contemporary events in Shakespeare's times and the symbolism first proposed in the fable of the belly.

47/53	Conflict
16/50	Feeding
47/52	Voices
46/53	Menenius

---

49 3 1 63 'Now as I live, I will. . . .'
Coriolanus feels provoked by the tribunes, and speaks his mind about the 'rank-scented meinie', characterizing them with a typical disease-image as 'measles'. Unlike Menenius, Coriolanus cannot flatter with words, or make them play tricks for him, and this is a mark of his integrity. Conversely, however, his stubbornness is a great disadvantage for someone so much in the political public eye. Is it unreasonable of us to expect politicians, as the citizenry do, to say what we wish to hear and yet keep honest? Is it not just a case of playing the appropriate part – something which Coriolanus admits he would 'blush' to do? Just as Coriolanus loses the consulship because he cannot change when necessary from soldier to politician, so he loses his life because he cannot change from being his mother's son to being his mother's soldier when it is appropriate.

30/50	Disease
45/55	Virtue
47/50	Citizens
47/51	Coriolanus

Characters and ideas
previous/next comment

50 3 1 154 '. . . at once pluck out/The multitudinous tongue: . . .'
This comment, with its reference to the citizens' tongues, and its echo of
their 'voices', strikes a note which was first introduced with the fable of the
belly. References to the human body and its parts as a parallel for the body-
politic occur throughout the play. No attempt has been made in this guide to
identify every one, although you should try to notice them when they do
occur and consider the allusions they create by their presence.

43/73   Body
49/51   Disease
48/51   Feeding
46/55   Power
49/52   Citizens
45/51   Tribunes

Again we see the notion that power, which is the 'sweet' referred to by
Coriolanus, will poison all of Rome if fed to the multitude. Notice how, time
and again, the patricians see Rome in terms of architecture and property – the
physical aspects of the body politic. Sicinius, as one of the people's tribunes,
identifies the perspective of the citizenry when he asks: 'What is the city but
the people?'. The common populace concern themselves with the more
mortal issue of feeding themselves, asking only 'For corn at their own rates,
whereof . . . the city is well stor'd.'

51 3 1 177 'Hence rotten thing! or I shall shake . . .'
Coriolanus consistently denigrates the plebeians; he despises everything
about them and, in fairness to him, you may sense that his feelings are
justified. But just as we might argue that Coriolanus's feelings in this matter
are a poison in the state of Rome, so they are a poison in Coriolanus himself,
and the ugliness of the poison is here revealed. As Brutus comments some
forty lines on, corrupted pride is 'very poisonous where the disease is
violent'.

50/59   Disease
50/66   Feeding
46/53   State
49/52   Coriolanus
50/53   Tribunes

Later still in this scene, Sicinius describes Coriolanus as 'a disease that must
be cut away' and calls him a limb that has become 'gangren'd'. Coriolanus is
a poison within the body of the State; he is death personified.

As in *Macbeth*, there is a further paradox here, for those very qualities for
which the hero is admired, honoured and ennobled are those which become
the greatest threat to the State's existence later on. Coriolanus's virtue, as
Wilson Knight observes, is the virtue of destruction which, because it has
been raised to its extreme, becomes divorced from love and therefore from
humanity: he becomes a death-phantom masquerading as life.

52 3 1 193 'Martius would have all from you, Martius . . .'
Although the citizenry have named Martius for consul, they had named him
by that time as Coriolanus, which makes the tribunes' omission of this name
all the more slighting. Given the connection between names and identity for
Martius in the play, this omission is a tacit suggestion that the tribunes will
not acknowledge the battle honour which now surrounds Coriolanus.

48/53   Voices
50/56   Citizens
51/54   Coriolanus

In this context it is interesting that, although the citizens mention Martius by
name in the first of the opening incidents in the play – and *may* mention his
battle-won name here, although this is unclear (3 1 185) – they never honour
him with 'Coriolanus', which is a title bestowed upon him by Cominius, a
general and his fellow nobleman. The plebeians' code of honour is therefore
distanced from that of the ruling warrior classes. A differing perception of
identity is reinforced by the use of names.

53 3 1 264 'He shall be thrown down the Tarpeian rock . . .'
This is the same rock referred to in Act three, scene three, and was a steep
cliff on one side of one of the seven hills of Rome. Traitors were flung to
their deaths from the top.

48/54   Conflict
51/56   State
8/55   Stone

All seem united in recognizing that Coriolanus must be stopped before things get completely out of hand. Menenius sees the problem as amenable to a cosmetic solution, something which can be resolved by the use of 'bolted language'. The tribunes see the matter as requiring a surgical solution: 'He's a disease that must be cut away'. Cominius perceives the threat to be to the 'falling fabric' of the State – an architectural allusion appropriate for a patrician (see note 50).

54 3 1 283 'For we are peremptory to dispatch . . .'
This is an interesting reference, and alludes to the folk-tale that the viper eats the womb from which it is born. Coriolanus therfore is attempting to destroy the city which gave him birth. At the end of the play (5 3 123) Volumnia accuses her son of marching 'to assault thy country' and compares it to treading on 'thy mother's womb'. Consider to what extent the viper-fable is paralleled in the relationship between Coriolanus, his mother and his son.

55 3 2 1 'Let them pull all about mine ears, . . .'
During this scene we see Coriolanus in rather petulant mood, unwilling to accept the necessity for any of the usual social graces. He again displays his contempt for those he sees as his inferiors in society, and once more we see him in unyielding mood. You should consider to what extent this is a legacy of his upbringing – how far his apparent pride and arrogance are merely echoes of his mother's views. You might even feel that Coriolanus's character is partly undeveloped and immature.

Volumnia herself sees no difficulty in dissembling for the voices of the public because, for her, Roman honour lies in those voices. Menenius and the other patricians have already tried and failed with this line of persuasion, but for his mother to urge it upon him confirms the insight of the two officers in Act two, scene two, that the patrician viewpoint is hopelessly hypocritical. Coriolanus is trapped by the political circumstances which surround him, by his upbringing and his birthright. The issue which so concerns Coriolanus – his relationship with his own inner voices of truth – is more than just irrelevant for Volumnia; she agrees with the mob that his objections to seeking their voices can be rooted only in pride.

The conflict in this scene is of course a result of Coriolanus's being unable to act the popular leader, because his upbringing has not prepared him for it. But notice how his mother forces him to humble himself before the Roman mob. This is the first of two blows (both delivered by his mother) which destroy him. Through her upbringing of her son, Volumnia has attempted to make him the embodiment of honour, and in this sense could be seen as the source of all his pride. It is therefore dramatically important that Volumnia is present on all three critical occasions in the action: when Coriolanus rejects the cloak of humility; when he refuses to bridle his feelings and dissemble to the mob so that he may be consul; and when he stands before Rome with the Volscian army at his side.

It is worth considering carefully the extent to which Coriolanus's character could be a product of his mother's inability to love him. She has raised him in pride to be the way he is, although she attempts to deny it in this scene:

'Thy valiantness was mine, thou suck'dst it from me,/But owe thy pride thyself.'

You should consider the extent to which Volumnia is as blameless as she argues. Does she love him, or just his glory? Notice she says how keen she would be to have a dead son, providing she could exchange his corpse for his 'good report'. Has she created a son who cannot be loved for himself,

and who cannot therefore love others? Notice how this view would accord
well with the mechanical 'engine' imagery which surrounds Coriolanus later
in the play. Does he become a machine, a robotic image of death incapable of
human feeling? Here he defies the plebeians to pull down the fabric of the
State upon him; a reference which echoes that of Cominius – see comment
53.

In *Macbeth*, the pursuit of ambition produces a retreat from humanity, and
alienates Lord and Lady Macbeth both from each other and from life. So too
do extreme pride and the pursuit of honour drive mother and son apart in
Coriolanus, the mother eventually siding with the plebeians she taught her
son to despise.

---

56 3 2 39 'You are too absolute. . . .'
In this paradoxical remark, Volumnia encapsulates the essential tragedy of
Coriolanus. His most characteristic comment is that he is 'constant', he will
not be false to his nature. The bewildering moral situation in the play is set
against the Elizabethan concept of a steady-state universe, with its checks,
its balances, its humours and its hierarchical view of creation. Within the
frequent metallic imagery of the play there are Elizabethan connotations of
baseness, of nobility and, most tellingly, of temper. Coriolanus's absolute
virtue may represent the essential quality of the play's Elizabethan-cum-
Roman world, but if it is untempered it cannot bend, and must perforce be
broken.

55/58	Conflict
40/85	Metal
53/57	State
55/59	Virtue
52/61	Citizens
54/59	Coriolanus
33/87	Virgilia
55/57	Volumnia

The problem in *Coriolanus* is that none of the groups within the Roman State
seem to discharge their responsibilities properly. The whole of this third act
of the play is a presentation of clashing theories of good government and
how different factions within the State should conduct themselves.
Coriolanus seems actively to hate the people, cursing them vilely on almost
every occasion he comes across them. In this, Coriolanus breaks every rule
of his age about the appropriate behaviour of leaders, rulers and kings. The
mob themselves are no less to blame, for the play opens with them in
uproar, at odds with the State. Menenius's fable of the belly pointedly
illustrates for the theatre audience the danger in this. The senate seem not to
care about the people. The tribunes seem more concerned with their own
status than with representing the citizens.

Coriolanus's mother sees her son vicariously, as something to generate ever
more honour. Of all the characters in the play, perhaps only Virgilia,
Coriolanus's wife, is without blame for the political débâcle.

---

57 3 2 62 'I would dissemble with my nature . . .'
Volumnia urges expediency upon her son, pointing out that his 'fortunes
and friends' are at stake. It is an appeal to caste rather than to patriotism,
although we might feel that Volumnia sees the two as synonymous. Later in
the play, in urging her son to a course of action which proves fatal to him,
she again appeals to him at a personal level rather than at the level of matters
of State. Do you think that Volumnia really sees her actions as patriotic? Is
this the only interpretation which makes sense of her final disregard for the
ties of family and caste? Does she ever really put personal motives of love
and revenge aside?

55/59	Dissembling
55/64	Power
56/61	State
56/58	Volumnia

---

58 3 2 72 'I prithee now, my son, . . .'
Volumnia pleads with her son and tries to teach him the part he should play
before the people. The concentration of the play's language upon action

56/59	Conflict
55/61	Voices

rather than upon expression has been pointed out earlier in this guide, and here we have Volumnia's confirmation that in *Coriolanus*, 'action is eloquence'. The 'ripest mulberry' simile is not an essential part of what Volumnia is saying, and her meaning would be as clear without it. This is often not the case in Shakespeare's other works, where the meaning of a passage *is* the simile which is used.

Unlike Shakespeare's other great tragic heroes, Coriolanus himself seems to have no fondness for or skill with words. This could, of course, be because of his aversion to falseness and flattery, but whatever the reason, it has implications for the use of language throughout the play. Menenius repeatedly tells us that the hero's 'heart's his mouth', and that he is 'ill school'd/In bolted language; meal and bran together/He throws without distinction'. Coriolanus is blunt; he says what is on his mind in the most direct manner he knows. This, ironically, is something Menenius always claims to do also, but if this is so, he does it with very different effect to Coriolanus. You may perhaps feel that Shakespeare deliberately avoided soliloquy in *Coriolanus*, as inappropriate to this unsubtle character. Notice, though, that it is Aufidius's mention of one word alone that precipitates Coriolanus's undoing.

---

59 3 2 120 'I will not do't, . . .'
In spite of the earlier urgings of Coriolanus's mother to 'perform a part/Thou hast not done before', and 'Go, and be rul'd', and of his agreement that he will do it, his sense of honour eventually rebels. Coriolanus is being asked to compromise, but he is being offered no moral alternative – he is being invited to betray his principles in the cause of what is practicable; he is being encouraged quite simply to back down.

58/61   Conflict
51/66   Disease
57/62   Dissembling
55/60   Pride
56/60   Virtue
56/60   Coriolanus

Coriolanus finally agrees to go to the market place only after his mother rebukes him for his pride. This is a crucial accusation – is Coriolanus guilty of pride? Certainly it is true that others in the play see this fault in him, and there is plenty of circumstantial evidence to support their view. Whether or not you accept this view will be central to the way you perceive what is really going on in the play. For example, do you judge Coriolanus to be proud because he cannot jettison his principles when they become inconvenient? Or do you feel that Coriolanus is playing the hypocrite in order to protect his ego?

The issue of Coriolanus's reluctance to seek the voices of those he later describes as 'curs', whose 'loves' he says 'I prize/As the dead carcasses of unburied men', is not one which we find raised in Plutarch. Shakespeare's most notable change of events and plot revolves around this issue, which passes unmentioned in his sources. For Plutarch, the Roman world of Coriolanus was a 'golden and vnfoiled age' and the voices of the populace 'whole in iudgement'. In Shakespeare's drama the voices of the people are meaningless for Coriolanus, for they are not uniformly good and incorruptible – indeed, they are repeatedly described by him in terms of corruption.

As Simmons points out, it is his conflicting allegiances to the two worlds – the real and the ideal – which makes Coriolanus and Rome finally incompatible.

---

60 3 3 25 'Put him to choler straight; . . .'
In this speech Brutus highlights a character defect in Coriolanus which is of crucial importance in his subsequent tragedy: 'Being once chaf'd, he cannot/ Be rein'd again to temperance'. Both of the occasions when Coriolanus is

'chaf'd' into losing his temper are disastrous for him – one results in his exile and the other in his death.

61 3 3 66 'For which you are a traitor . . .'

This is the crucial turning-point in the play, as Coriolanus is named as traitor, not consul. With this the State is thrown into a moral chaos, for when the rabble are given the power to judge and condemn Coriolanus, they are condemning that which has already been acknowledged as the cornerstone of the Capitol; and which has been depicted as the essential foundation and *virtus* of Rome. Plutarch also argued that the voice of the mob, if vested with power, would eventually destroy civilization.

59/62	Conflict
47/62	Creatures
57/65	State
55/65	Stone
60/65	Virtue
58/62	Voices
56/63	Citizens
60/63	Coriolanus

During the Renaissance the best form of government was generally held to be a monarchy; next best an aristocracy; and worst a democracy. The Elizabethans' fear of democracy may seem odd to us, but it was founded in the belief that a democratic society would inevitably degenerate into chaos because of the mob's essentially fickle and contrary nature. For example, in the third scene of Act two the citizenry recall that for the populace to be ungrateful is monstrous; it makes 'a monster of the multitude'. The citizens recollect their common name of 'the many-headed multitude' and the image of the all-devouring Hydra is complete; it is further exemplified when they aver that 'if all our wits were to issue out of one skull, they would fly east, west, north, south, and their consent of one direct way should be at once to all the points o'th'compass.' Two proclamations made in 1607 suggest that *Coriolanus* had hit a recognized mark:

> It is a thing notorious that many of the meanest sort of our people . . . have presumed lately to assemble themselves riotously in multitudes . . . the glory and strength of all kings consisteth in the multitude of subjects.
>
> *(28th June 1607)*

> Of all other seditions and rebellions none doth bring such infinite waste and desolation upon a kingdom or state as these popular insurrections, which though they do seldom shake or endanger a crown, yet they do bring a heap of calamities upon multitudes of innocent subjects, and chiefly upon the authors and actors themselves.
>
> *(24th July 1607)*

62 3 3 120 'You common cry of curs! . . .'

This powerful speech is a prophetic and, in many ways, an accurate summary of the situation. Notice the parallels between the way this scene ends and the way the play ends – both have an ungrateful populace 'hooting out' their past hero because he will not 'temporize' with them, and subsequently living to regret their haste. There are several occasions in the play when Coriolanus is rejected by others because he will not become what they wish him to; he will not allow them to 'pay' him for his exploits in their own coin. Depending on the point of view adopted, this can be seen as either Coriolanus's greatest weakness, or his greatest strength. What exactly did Volumnia want her son to become? What did the plebeians want him to become? What did Aufidius want him to become? Did any of these people care what Coriolanus's own wishes were? What did Coriolanus himself want to become?

61/66	Conflict
61/63	Creatures
59/64	Dissembling
43/77	Payment
61/71	Voices

Act 4

63 4 1 15 'I shall be lov'd when I am lack'd. . . .'
Do you detect any radical change in Coriolanus by this point? Would the Coriolanus of Acts one, two and three have used the word 'lov'd'? Is Coriolanus suggesting that the Roman mob may come to 'love' him – or has he his own mother in mind? In either case, do you think that perhaps Coriolanus needs the affection and support of others more than he had thought?

Contrast this parting with their next meeting, where Coriolanus sees things very differently and says that his eyes 'are not the same I wore in Rome'. The reference here to a dragon emphasizes Coriolanus's current isolation, and also contrasts with the next allusions to the beast, where Aufidius says he 'fights dragon-like' and Menenius that he 'has wings' and is 'grown from man to dragon'. Such contrasts echo throughout a play so full of reversals, to underpin the rise and fall of the tragic hero.

64 4 2 34 'Cats, that can judge as fitly . . .'
Now that Volumnia's silence can help Coriolanus no further, she sees no cause to hold her tongue. You should consider to what extent her pride is as great as that of her son, but simply better hidden. Volumnia seems to be a strong and determined woman, with a good grasp of politics and intrigue. Whether we could go so far as to agree with those who see her as a woman to be wondered at, rather than liked, is another matter – particularly as they go on to say that she is a masculine type who would have been happier in the world as a man!

65 4 2 39 'As far as doth the Capitol exceed . . .'
In Volumnia's eyes, Coriolanus symbolizes the essential and permanent qualities of Rome; he is a monolith, rising above the base, the mean, the vulgar, and the despised mob. The metaphors identifying Coriolanus's virtues with the permanence of architecture recur throughout the play. Notice Menenius's observation in the fourth scene of Act five, where he asks Sicinius whether he can see the corner-stone of the Capitol, for:

> If it be possible for you to displace it with your
> little finger, there is some hope the ladies of Rome,
> especially his mother, may prevail with him. But I
> say there is no hope in't; . . .

Coriolanus is steadfast in upholding those values which are portrayed as the literal foundations of the State. Interestingly, this leaves Shakespeare's play at odds with Plutarch, where Coriolanus's ultimate failure is explained instead as being largely due to his lack of formal schooling:

> . . . for lacke of education, he was so chollericke and
> impacient, that he would yeld to no living creature:
> which made him churlishe, uncivill, and altoghether
> unfit for any mans conversation.

Plutarch grants Coriolanus a 'great harte' and acknowledges that it encouraged him 'to doe and attempt notable actes'. But Plutarch also points out that the historical Coriolanus lacked the benefit of that learning which 'teacheth men that be rude and rough of nature, by compasse and rule of reason, to be civill &. curteous, and to like better the meane state, then the higher'.

The tragedy of Shakespeare's Coriolanus is that his uncompromising virtue, depicted as the essence of Roman civilization, is paradoxically that which

Characters and ideas	
previous/next comment	
55/69	Child
62/64	Creatures
61/65	Citizens
61/64	Coriolanus
58/64	Volumnia
63/76	Creatures
62/67	Dissembling
57/68	Power
60/78	Pride
63/65	Coriolanus
63/65	Volumnia
61/68	State
61/87	Stone
61/67	Virtue
63/75	Citizens
64/68	Coriolanus
64/66	Volumnia

brings him down – he is destroyed by hubris. Coriolanus's all-embracing *virtus* positively excludes all else, including life itself, as Volumnia perceived in the second scene of Act three: 'You are too absolute'.

From a purely technical point of view, this scene is important in pushing Volumnia more centre-stage in the absence of her son. She has already had a large part to play in his achievements in battle and in his banishment, and now we are being prepared for her third and greatest intervention in the fate of her son.

66 4 2 50 'Anger's my meat: I sup upon myself . . .'

Volumnia, like her son, feeds on herself, and in so doing her emotions literally eat away at her from within. As the action of *Coriolanus* illustrates, extremes of love, pride, honour – and by implication other passions – consume themselves, in their attempts to prolong their own lives, in fires of their own making. Thus Coriolanus's desire at the start of Act five is to have 'forg'd himself a name o'th'fire of burning Rome'.

62/67	Conflict
59/76	Disease
51/71	Feeding
65/78	Volumnia

Volumnia's incessant striving for honour for her son leads her to label him a traitor, and him to turn destructively upon the city which has made him what he is. The 'feeding' imagery resurfaces tellingly at the opening of Act five, as Coriolanus enters the house of Aufidius during a feast, to join him in opposition to Rome.

67 4 3 1 'I know you well, sir, . . .'

This brief scene parallels that found at the start of Act two, scene two – both serve a semi-choric function, by drawing together in a balanced way the key strands of the current situation. In addition, the present scene reinforces our understanding, gained in the first act, of how much each side knows about the other's military and political situation, although here the intelligence travels one way only. The Roman traitor Nicanor speaks of patricians and plebeians as man and wife, and notes that 'the fittest time to corrupt a man's wife is when she's fallen out with her husband' – the multiple meaning of 'corrupt' including 'seditious' as well as 'lacking in integrity'. The defection of Nicanor pre-empts that of another Roman, Coriolanus, both in the action and in the allusions in his remarks.

66/70	Conflict
64/69	Dissembling
55/99	Service
65/77	Virtue

68 4 4 12 'O world, thy slippery turns! . . .'

The use of soliloquy in *Coriolanus* is minimal; the play has less than forty lines, altogether, which puts it on a par with *As You Like It*, in having fewer than any other of Shakespeare's plays. This illustrates the lack of introspection in the play, the emphasis on the public world of affairs rather than the private, inward world of the hero. Contrast this with *Macbeth*, where we gain insight into many of the characters through their soliloquies. The most extreme contrast would be with *Hamlet*, where the hero adopts soliloquy almost as his normal mode of expression.

64/72	Power
65/70	State
65/69	Coriolanus

Here the loneliness of Coriolanus is emphasized – his spiritual exile as a traitor. His isolation on stage in a play so full of the action of battle and the bustle of the city and the Senate would also make a strong dramatic point, perhaps a more telling visual image than those embedded in the language. Consider how far this use of imagery in the play is more appropriate to its form.

69 4 4 12 'O world, thy slippery turns! . . .'
This is Coriolanus's one soliloquy in the play. At this stage he is the 'lonely dragon', the man of constancy in a fickle world which has banished him as a public enemy for his services to the State. Interestingly, for the first time we find Coriolanus without a perceived identity; he is 'in mean apparel, disguised and muffled'. This description may owe less to Shakespeare's stage directions than to additions by later editors, although, in this particular case, North's Plutarch is followed closely:

> For he disguised him selfe in suche arraye and
> attire, as he thought no man could ever have knowen
> him for the persone he was . . .

Within the context of the play, Coriolanus is losing contact with his original identity of Caius Martius, and is moving towards becoming the nameless terror of Act five. The importance of true identity is well scored in the next scene in this act.

63/76	Child
67/70	Dissembling
68/70	Coriolanus

70 4 4 23 'My birthplace hate I, . . .'
Unlike Shakespeare's other great tragic figures, Coriolanus speaks no great soliloquy prior to this moment. We are given no inner view to explain how this behaviour came about. By the time Coriolanus speaks these words, the moment has passed, the decision is fixed, and no trace of its making can be found in the text. This emphasizes to us the nature of the character of Coriolanus: we see inbred convictions, we see impulsive decisions, we see morality at its blackest and whitest, but we see no process by which this has happened, no internal moral conflicts, no writhings with conscience – nothing. Coriolanus does not argue himself into this position, or find it growing within him slowly, as might Hamlet or Macbeth, for example.

67/72	Conflict
69/71	Dissembling
68/81	State
69/71	Coriolanus

71 4 5 54 'Whence com'st thou? What wouldst thou? . . .'
Shakespeare emphasizes the importance of names here. The scene opened, as the last one closed, with Coriolanus having moved from Caius Martius to self-imposed anonymity. Here the theme is more explicitly developed, with Aufidius repeatedly asking the name of this figure before him. Martius confesses that all that now remains of his old self has gone – it has been 'devoured' – and he has only the surname 'Coriolanus', which has become 'witness of the malice and displeasure/Which thou should'st bear me.' Coriolanus has come to Antium, not so much in search of revenge, as in search of who he is. Is the progressive renaming of Martius throughout the play reflected by a progressive restructuring of his character – or do you feel that he remains consistent throughout?

70/75	Dissembling
66/77	Feeding
62/72	Voices
25/73	Aufidius
70/72	Coriolanus

72 4 5 196 'Why, he is so made on here within . . .'
The third Servingman continues: 'as if he were son and heir to Mars', and this association of Coriolanus's own name of Caius Martius with that of Mars is revealing. Coriolanus appeals to the god Mars on two important occasions in the play – one at the start of the play outside the walls of Corioli: 'Now Mars, I prithee make us quick in work'; and the other at the end of the play, when he appeals to the god after Aufidius taunts him because he spared Rome: 'Hears't thou, Mars?' Aufidius himself refers to Coriolanus as 'thou Mars' as he welcomes him into his house (4 5 119), and later in the same scene the servants note that he is treated by the Volsces 'as if he were the son and heir to Mars'.

This preoccupation with the name of the hero is important, because it reflects upon his *identity*. He is who his name says he is, and the 'boy' jibe at the end of the play has a profound effect because of this. The names by

70/73	Conflict
68/74	Power
71/81	Voices

which Caius Martius is known throughout the play are more than metaphorical, they are almost alchemical. At each turn of the action we see not so much different sides to one whole character being revealed, as different characters seeming to emerge from the chrysalis of the preceding one. The child-warrior becomes warrior-myth; the mythic-hero becomes demi-god; and the vengeful spirit of death is rendered mortal again by the powerful incantation of Volumnia.

The tragedy of Coriolanus is that the price of regaining his humanity is his life – it is more the tragedy of a man who falls *to* grace than one who falls *from* grace. There is also a trace of this theme in each of the four great tragedies written between 1601 and 1606: *Hamlet, Othello, King Lear*, and *Macbeth*.

73 4 5 199 'Our general himself/makes a mistress of him, . . .'
Here the servants continue the sexual imagery of the previous scene. Some critics have interpreted Shakespeare's use of this kind of imagery as hinting at a sexual relationship between Aufidius and Coriolanus – at least, a sexual relationship expressed in terms of the physical exertion and intimate contact of battle. Certainly we might agree with those critics who have observed that, for Coriolanus and Aufidius, the act of war is a majestic and thrilling ecstasy. This interpretation of the play does not rely on an exclusively modern theme in literature, although you might more readily expect to come across it in modern works, such as those of D.H. Lawrence.

50/74	Body
72/74	Conflict
71/78	Aufidius
72/75	Coriolanus

74 4 5 233 '. . . and as wars, in some sort, may be . . .'
Those critics who have argued that sex is depicted in *Coriolanus* as an alternative to war, and vice versa, sometimes cite this conversation among the three Servingmen. There are many other examples in the play, some of which you will find drawn to your attention in other parts of these critical notes.

73/90	Body
73/77	Conflict
40/78	Domination
72/76	Power

The idea that war is a sexual displacement-activity – a kind of communal or group therapy – was not a new one, even in Shakespeare's day. The notion that war somehow bonds together individuals on all sides can be found as readily in modern Western art as in Greek drama. The Freudian proposition that this bonding is an expression, or displacement, of the sexual urge to dominate others may be only a modern formulation of a long-recognized feature of human relations. In the next scene, Cominius, whilst extending the Servingmen's imagery, also details the immediate consequences for the citizenry of this: 'You have holp to ravish your own daughters, . . .'.

75 4 6 27 'This is a happier and more comely time . . .'
Sicinius argues that, without Coriolanus, things are better, but this view by the people's tribune should be contrasted with the insight shown earlier by the people themselves in the previous scene, where we find one observing acutely that peace 'makes men hate one another' because 'they then less need one another'. This scene is almost a parody of the first scene in the play. The harmonius good-fellowship is overdone and almost hypocritical. Is there any dramatic reason why this might be deliberate?

71/77	Dissembling
65/76	Citizens
73/76	Coriolanus
53/77	Tribunes

Whilst it would be easy to explain how Rome might need Coriolanus during times of strife, how might you argue that Coriolanus needs Rome? In what sense does Coriolanus rely on Rome for his identity? Why could we say that his move to the Volscian camp was, in this regard, doomed to failure?

Do you feel that the tribunes are unrelievedly scurrilous? Evidence that they are capable of being even-handed and almost noble can be found later in this scene, where Sicinius counsels the citizens to go home, and again near the start of scene one of Act five, where he urges Menenius to go and see Coriolanus, saying that even if he is unsuccessful, Rome will honour his good intentions. However, in fairness, the weight of evidence seems set on the side of the tribunes' poorer qualities.

76 4 6 91 'He is their god. He leads them . . .'
Coriolanus approaches as the lord of death. Again, he is shown as far exceeding all other men in his qualities – he is of a higher order and is a 'god'. Notice how he speaks of Rome as 'canker'd' – the disease imagery interestingly reversed in its application here.

69/86	Child
64/77	Creatures
66/0	Disease
74/80	Power
75/77	Citizens
75/77	Coriolanus

Also present in this speech is an interesting reference to the theme of children, which links with an earlier incident involving Coriolanus's son and also with the boy's only speech in Act five:

> . . . and they follow him
> Against us brats, with no less confidence
> Than boys pursuing summer butterflies,
> Or butchers killing flies.

Compare the imagery in this speech with 1 3 57 and 5 3 127. Tellingly, the citizenry of Rome have become 'flies', and the full-grown Coriolanus a 'butcher'.

77 4 6 100 'He'll shake your Rome about your ears.'
The hypocrisy of the plebeians is well observed in this scene, as we see all about dissembling. Notice how every character affirms that they acted to banish Coriolanus only in reluctance, or in deference to the wishes of others. Could we argue that only the tribunes are consistent here?

74/79	Conflict
76/80	Creatures
75/79	Dissembling
71/80	Feeding
62/0	Payment
67/79	Virtue
76/95	Citizens
76/78	Coriolanus
75/96	Tribunes

The reference to Hercules and the 'mellow fruit' is apposite. Hercules's eleventh labour (of the twelve) was to fetch the golden apples guarded by the Hesperides, the 'daughters of evening'. The apples were continually watched by a dragon called Ladon. The garden of the Hesperides was variously placed near Mount Atlas, in the extreme west, or in Arcadia. Hercules had to bear the weight of heaven whilst Atlas agreed to go for the apples for him. Some legends have it that Hercules also slew the hundred-headed dragon, Ladon. Consider the interesting parallels between the labours of Hercules and those of Coriolanus: the apples and valour, and Ladon and 'The beast/With many heads' which butts Coriolanus away – the first scene in Act four rewards study in this context.

78 4 7 8 'He bears himself more proudlier . . .'
Aufidius's subsequent actions and motives are justified specifically only by this one item, and this would support the argument that a basic part of the human make-up is the urge to dominate. Look at the words spoken at various points by Volumnia and Coriolanus himself for further evidence of this.

74/97	Domination
64/79	Pride
73/79	Aufidius
77/79	Coriolanus
66/86	Volumnia

79 4 7 28 'All places yields to him . . .'
This speech by Aufidius has drawn much critical comment, not least because of the half-soliloquy feel it has. Coleridge saw the speech as an 'imperfection'. Suppose we have the Lieutenant answered with a dismissive wave at line twenty-seven, and withdrawing slightly to leave Aufidius alone with the audience. Consider the differing dramatic effects created with, and then without, the Lieutenant listening.

77/81	Conflict
77/84	Dissembling
78/89	Pride
77/80	Virtue
78/85	Aufidius
78/80	Coriolanus

In this speech Aufidius, who cannot bring himself to name 'him', identifies a mixture of ruling passions which together consistute Coriolanus's tragic flaw: 'defect of judgement' combines with his inflexible nature and his failure to take 'those chances which he was lord of', with the result that he is 'feared . . . hated, and so banished'. Significantly, Aufidius concentrates on the inflexible qualities of Coriolanus, which ill-befit him for civil life. Coriolanus cannot change his nature to suit times of peace – he is the absolute warrior, the 'flower of warriors', whose sword is 'death's stamp'. He cannot, therefore, change his manner as he moves 'From th'casque to th'cushion'. Aufidius recognizes that this will be his undoing:

> One fire drives out one fire; one nail one nail;
> Rights by rights falter, strengths by strengths do fail.

Coriolanus will be forced to choose between two goods, and that will be his tragedy. At the moment when Coriolanus's mother has 'won a happy victory to Rome', but one 'most mortal' to her son, Aufidius makes his meaning clear in his aside.

> I am glad thou hast set thy mercy and thy
> honour
> At difference in thee. Out of that I'll work
> Myself a former fortune.

(5 3 200)

80 4 7 33 'I think he'll be to Rome . . .'
Notice how the aristocratic, almost god-like, authority of Coriolanus is emphasized at every turn. The osprey was deemed to be such a noble bird that the fish turned up their glittering undersides and sacrificed themselves to it. The implication is that Coriolanus's nobility should command supplication from the plebeians by a similar force of moral and natural right. Whether the osprey's fish, or Coriolanus's citizenry, accept this role becomes the point at issue. It is not the right of nobility to be regarded as superior which is under dispute, but the manner in which the mantle of superiority should be worn.

Notice the implication here that Coriolanus will 'devour' Rome; that Rome must be sacrificed in order to preserve the existence of Coriolanus. This allusion anticipates one mentioned in comment 81, that Coriolanus will recreate himself from the burning embers of Rome.

77/81   Creatures
77/82   Feeding
76/87   Power
79/84   Virtue
79/81   Coriolanus

Act 5

81 5 1 11 '"Coriolanus"/He would not answer to; . . .'
Where is the world in which Coriolanus belongs? Is this not the problem we sense in the play? Away from Rome, Coriolanus becomes nothing; only in the 'fire of burning Rome' can he rise, phoenix-like, with a new identity. The drama is one in which we find, confusingly, a public hero who has no public.

We see Coriolanus becoming totally de-humanized. Given the role of names in the play, his rejection of all names implies the rejection of all identity. He has become nothing – a wraith, an all-consuming empty void – he has become Death. He is to 'forge himself a name o'th'fire/Of burning Rome'. Coriolanus, the 'thing of blood', is now to become a thing of fire, to emerge reborn from the ruins of his old life. It is in this scene, where his spirit is poised on the edge of the abyss, between the realms of deity and demon, that his mother calls out to him. Whatever the outcome the point at issue is whether he will be destroyed by his rejection of his mortality, or by his acceptance of it.

82 5 1 47 'I'll undertake't. . . .'
Menenius seems almost to gloat at the failure of Cominius, and makes much of the predicament that the tribunes have created for them all. His speech here seems inappropriately pompous and verbose, and his tendency to metaphor, so successful at the start of the play in the fable of the belly, seems to fall flat here.

Menenius assumes that Coriolanus rejected Cominius because 'he had not dined', which is an interesting echo of the food imagery at the start of the play. Menenius appears arrogant in his assumption that he will catch Coriolanus in a better mood than did Cominius. Has Menenius been shallow and smug all along? Has he consistently overrated his own importance and influence? Apart from the plebeians, who are swayed by slippery tongues on several occasions, does Menenius ever influence anyone?

Notice here how Cominius recognizes that Coriolanus, whose eye was 'Red as 'twould burn Rome', will not be easily swayed. Cominius has not abused the tribunes, and seems genuinely to have the future of Rome as his only concern. We might feel that Menenius, by contrast, will turn whatever occasion he can to his personal advantage.

83 5 1 63 'I tell you, he does sit in gold, . . .'
Notice how the imagery of burning becomes increasingly frequent as the play moves towards its close. The fire is to be cathartic: a cleansing, a purging of both the body politic and the souls of men.

84 5 2 1 'Stay! Whence are you?'
This scene opens with Menenius discovering that his offices – and more importantly, given the significance of this in the play, his name – no longer carry weight. He has become a nothing: 'the virtue of your name/Is not here passable', says the guard. The wheel of fortune turns for others in the play as well as for Coriolanus, and Menenius finds that pride does indeed precede a fall. Menenius tells the guard that he is a great friend of Coriolanus, but notice how the guard observes that Menenius is notorious for his own self-adulation:

Faith, sir, if you had told as many lies in
his behalf as you have uttered words in your own,
you should not pass here; . . .

85 5 2 92 'You keep a constant temper.'

Aufidius's cryptic remark is full of double meaning. Coriolanus does indeed
keep his 'temper' constantly on the brink of boiling, and in other respects
also keeps faith with his own character, and in that sense also is 'constant'.
The suggestion of a metallic 'temper' is also important here, and one which
is common in Shakespeare. Why then are we unconvinced? Does Aufidius
seem convinced? It is Coriolanus's manner which Shakespeare skilfully uses
to signal that he is wavering – we have the blustering dismissal, tempered
with the gift of a letter which he 'would have sent', but did not; we have the
situation itself, which seems staged to demonstrate his iron will to Aufidius;
and we have the ironic reference to Coriolanus as 'the oak not to be windshaken', when in the past he has been 'a harvest man' whose brows were
'bound with oak'.

84/88	Dissembling
56/89	Metal
84/86	Virtue
79/94	Aufidius
81/86	Coriolanus

86 5 3 8 'This last old man, . . .'

Coriolanus is not depicted as a character totally without human feeling, for
here he has tried to soften the blow of his rejection of Menenius. Earlier, we
have seen Coriolanus's gentleness towards his wife and mother, and also his
care for the poor old man who tended him in Corioli.

The important issue is that of Coriolanus's intentions in all this. For
example, how far can we really believe that he intended to destroy Rome?
Does not his wavering over Menenius's appeal belie this? And what of his
reaction at the news that his wife and mother are coming – does this suggest
to us that an iron will is at work? On the other hand, why should Coriolanus
return with Aufidius, to what he seems to acknowledge as his certain death,
when he could have entered Rome as its saviour? Surely we cannot believe
that Coriolanus does this because entering Rome might mean accepting
thanks from the plebeians? Even for Coriolanus, we might feel that this is
taking simple stubbornness too far, and that greater and more noble
sentiments are holding sway.

Interestingly, in view of Coriolanus's observation that Menenius loved him
'above the measure of a father', we hear no mention of Coriolanus's father,
and his mother's attitude may be the more understandable for that. Also
worth noting is the fact that Menenius seems to be the only character who
can chide Coriolanus, without the latter losing his temper as a result. In
many ways we could see Menenius as the consummate politician in all this,
whose interests are those of the State. You might also consider how far this
accolade could be extended to Volumnia who, in spite of her more abrasive
nature, arguably has the interests of the State above all else, in so far as she
seems prepared to sacrifice her own son for it if needs be.

76/89	Child
81/90	State
85/87	Virtue
85/87	Coriolanus
84/96	Menenius
78/89	Volumnia

87 5 3 29 'My mother bows,/As if Olympus . . .'

Coriolanus's speeches in this scene contain several classical references; here
in a simile comparing his mother to Olympus, the abode of the gods; later in
metaphor describing Valeria as Diana, the virginal Roman goddess of the
hunt and the moon; and then invoking 'the god of soldiers' (Mars) and Jove
in support of the warrior's 'nobleness' which is 'to shame invulnerable'. The
metaphoric imagery of stone now has Volumnia characterized as a
mountain, where Coriolanus has until now been compared to the
architecture of the State.

83/88	Conflict
80/89	Power
65/89	Stone
86/89	Virtue
86/88	Coriolanus
56/93	Virgilia

These references to absolute authority have something of the quality of an incantation – Coriolanus is trying to resist persuasion by his mother. He wishes to dehumanize himself, to cut off 'the access to remorse', as Lady Macbeth puts it in a scene with interesting parallels to this one. He wishes to be 'author of himself' and acknowledge 'no other kin'. Notice the completely different tenor of his speech after he relents.

The play can be seen as an affirmation of those human qualities which eventually are the undoing of Coriolanus – or the making of him, depending on your point of view. His comments at line twenty-seven may be more than just dramatic irony:

> What is that curtsy worth? or those doves' eyes,
> Which can make gods forsworn? . . .

At this point in the play Virgilia comes forward and uncharacteristically initiates the next section of the play's action. The appropriateness of this lies in the role which 'gracious silence' is about to play on the stage.

If we accept that Coriolanus is aware of the situation which fate and his nature have between them conspired to entrap him in, we may feel that *Coriolanus* is a tragedy in the traditional mould after all, and that we have sufficient emotional insight into the central character to allow us to feel pity. Coriolanus's speech, 'O world, thy slippery turns!' in scene four of Act four, could be used as good evidence that he recognizes and accepts the will of fate, but there is evidence within the text for views either way.

---

88 5 3 36 'As if a man were author of himself/And knew no other kin.'
These famous and crucial lines in the play encapsulate the central problem which Coriolanus now finds himself facing. In order to maintain his identity as the mythic warrior-god he must entirely renounce the last shreds of his humanity.

The rising power of Coriolanus's name in the play is underscored much earlier by his proud mother: 'What is it? – Coriolanus, must I call thee?' (2 1 173). As the action proceeds, his name becomes a talisman, with a force and power of its own. It is a thing of 'witchcraft', according to Aufidius's Lieutenant (4 7 2) which 'soldiers use . . . as the grace 'fore meat' at their meals.

The use of characters almost as tokens is perhaps one of the things which distances us from them in *Coriolanus*. How far do you think that this 'objectification' of character and use of somewhat de-personalized 'token' figures is a weakness in the play? Is it a necessary device, given Shakespeare's aims, as you perceive them? Consider to what extent this makes *Coriolanus* a moral fable rather than a dramatic tragedy, and think about how far we could fairly say that what Shakespeare actually wrote was not a drama of his usual kind, but more of a political morality play.

87/90	Conflict
85/90	Dissembling
82/98	Voices
87/89	Coriolanus

---

89 5 3 56 'What's this?/Your knees to me? . . .'
This scene contains many images of metal and stone intermixed with 'body' references. This is important, for Coriolanus eventually yields to the entreaty of 'great nature', expressed later in Volumnia's powerful speech beginning 'Should we be silent . . .'. Volumnia places herself between Coriolanus and his warrior-honour, and forces him to choose between this and 'thy mother's womb/That brought thee to this world.' Notice how she has seen her love for him: like a hen who 'Has cluck'd thee to the wars, and safely home,/Loaden with honour'. When even this fails, she turns his own pride against itself and, for a second time, her scornfulness wins him over:

86/91	Child
81/90	Creatures
85/0	Metal
87/97	Power
79/93	Pride
87/0	Stone
87/92	Virtue
88/91	Coriolanus
86/91	Volumnia

'This fellow had a Volscian to his mother; . . .'. For pride and honour must finally bow to the greatest god – Love; this is a recurrent theme found throughout Shakespeare's work: the warmth of love has triumphed where weapons and hard metallic pride have failed.

This is the second blow which Volumnia delivers to her son, and it is the one which destroys him: he returns to die in Antium, a traitor both to the Volscians and to Rome. But Coriolanus has not betrayed himself in this. The speech where he renounces pride and affirms his love for his mother is among Shakespeare's most powerful in its emotional intensity. For Coriolanus, and through him for us also, this is catharsis; he has been cleansed by his acceptance of genuine love in place of his pride-nobility. He has finally achieved by renunciation what he could not achieve by strife: an ultimate 'true' nobility. This is the Christian ethic which, throughout the play, is implicitly set against the pagan ethos of Rome and which makes *Coriolanus* a powerful explication of its historical fall.

If we can accept the fate of Coriolanus as that of a spirit victorious in death and glorious in its purity, then his final speech will hold no echo of past pride, but will strike us as a cry of glorious triumph:

> If you have writ your annals true, 'tis there,
> That like an eagle in a dove-cote, I
> Flutter'd your Volscians in Corioles.
> Alone I did it.

> (5 6 113)

90 5 3 101 'Making the mother, wife and child to see . . .'

Menenius's fable resurfaces again here, with an image of Coriolanus as son, husband and father 'tearing/His country's bowels out.' The image recurs throughout the play in different forms: we see Rome tearing itself apart with civil strife; the different factions within the body politic constantly at each other's throats; the warrior-code of honour confusing loyalties and personal ambitions within the soldiers and generals alike. Coriolanus himself is torn several ways by the calls of the competing members of his own peer-group and by the conflict within his own personality. Volumnia is only partly accurate in her wrath; the rest is irony – Coriolanus, like the body in the fable of the belly, is the one who will feed upon himself (an echo of Volumnia's reference, discussed in comment 66) and tear his own bowels out.

74/0	Body
88/91	Conflict
89/91	Creatures
88/92	Dissembling
82/0	Feeding
86/99	State

91 5 3 127 'A shall not tread on me. . . .'

Coriolanus's son is not an incidental addition to the action of the play. We have seen, in Volumnia's 'breasts of Hecuba' speech, the mingling of references to birth, motherhood, wounds and children. Also we have been shown how young Martius, in a temper at falling over chasing a butterfly, tears it to pieces with his teeth in 'one on's father's moods'. The boy is a developing theme throughout the play, set in counterpoint against the relationship between Coriolanus and his mother. There is something child-like (childish?) in Coriolanus's preoccupation with honour and bravery, and his stubbornness, temper and impetuosity, which is eloquently reflected in his son's single speech:

> A shall not tread on me.
> I'll run away till I am bigger, but then I'll fight.

89/92	Child
90/93	Conflict
90/95	Creatures
89/93	Coriolanus
89/92	Volumnia

This emphasis can also be found in the childish arguments of the plebeians, and in the way Menenius has to tell them a fable to ensure that they will understand him. Notice here that young Martius promises to become like his father. You may detect the hint that the cycle of fate could be about to run again, with Volumnia herself bringing up the boy in the absence of his father.

92 5 3 172 'So, we will home to Rome . . .'

In this long speech Volumnia uses the same technique which persuaded Coriolanus back to the forum – she appeals to his honour and patriotism. But how far does she employ emotional blackmail? Consider whether she is only pretending to admit defeat so that she can introduce images of him destroying his mother, wife and child. Is her self-sacrificing image of herself as a 'poor hen' convincing? Notice how she points out that 'the end of war's uncertain' but then offers him a certain ending with honour on all sides – providing, of course, that the Volscians are magnanimous in victory. Her speech is a brilliant mixture of appeals to his warrior-code, his patriotism and his humanity. By its end, she has said all there is to say and, briefly but appropriately, Coriolanus responds only with silence.

93 5 3 182 (*Holds her by the hand silent.*) . . .

This is the play's most tragic moment, where Coriolanus accepts defeat and impending death, both by his mother's hand. Such moments of silence are used with pointedness in Shakespeare's later plays, and are often marked by very specific stage directions, as here, or explicitly by the action – as when Macbeth hears of his wife's death, or as when Othello strikes Desdemona. Importantly here, we see that the conflict is resolved in the 'gracious silence' we have come to associate with Virgilia. Can you now assess the indirect influence she has exerted over the action of the play, and her importance as a character?

Given the use of language in the play and the relationship between imagery, action and Coriolanus, it is appropriate that his symbolic yielding should be in dumb-show. His silence now expresses not hardness and bluntness, but mercy. In Shakespeare's other tragedies we see the hero at the height of his eloquence as the tragedy reaches its climax, but with Coriolanus we find, as Volumnia said, that 'action is eloquence'; he holds his mother's hand in silence. His isolation from his mother, humanity and therefore from the humanity in himself has finally been broken.

An alternative view of this scene is that Coriolanus's conscience forces him to choose his own death, rather than that of his mother. He therefore accepts his death as the only alternative to matricide. But because Volumnia knows the implications for her son of the course she has driven him to, she commits a form of murder. Consider whether you accept the view that by sending him to battle at sixteen, for example, by glorying in his wounds, by seeing him solely as a vehicle for improving her own esteem, she has not all along subconsciously been attempting to destroy him.

From a dramatic point of view, the death of Coriolanus is essential. The Aristotelian theory of tragedy calls for the hero to fall to the depths from a great height and, given the context of the play, for the warrior character Coriolanus this cannot mean leaving him alive. But whilst we might be able to feel sorrow for the fall of Hamlet, of Macbeth and of Lear, can we feel this for the fall of Coriolanus? If Coriolanus were to be held guilty of absolutely unmitigated arrogance and pride it would be hard for us to feel genuinely sorry for him. You should therefore consider very carefully how Shakespeare avoided giving us this simplistic view, if indeed you think he did. Is it possible for the audience to see the pride of Coriolanus as a weakness in him, an effect of his perhaps over-zealous mother's upbringing of him, or simply as a reflection of his immaturity and impatience? What evidence from the play could you point to in support of such propositions?

94 5 3 194 'I was mov'd withal.'
This comment by Aufidius is all the more eloquent for its brevity. Since
Aufidius's semi-soliloquy with his Lieutenant, we have been aware of his
ultimate intention, and his mere presence is all that is now necessary to
remind us of this. Shakespeare does not enlarge upon characters any more
than is necessary and, like Virgilia, the watchful presence of Aufidius is
often enough to remind us of the dramatic tensions surrounding them.

92/98	Dissembling
85/98	Aufidius

95 5 4 11 'There is differency between . . .'
Here and throughout the play there is a continual contrast between *things*,
often between weak and strong things in nature; this is a parallel to the
contrast between Coriolanus and the citizenry. These contrasts, often
involving animals, occur in pairs: in the first scene of the play we find foxes
and geese, lions and hares, and oaks and rushes; scene three has men and
geese; scene four, the cat and the mouse; scene eight, weeds before a
vessel's keel; and so on throughout the other acts in the play. There are
many similar examples, and you will have little difficulty in finding them in
almost every scene.

93/96	Conflict
91/96	Creatures
93/98	Virtue
77/0	Citizens
93/97	Coriolanus

Coriolanus finds his equal only in his enemy, Aufidius:

> I sin in envying his nobility;
> And were I anything but what I am,
> I would wish me only he.

(1 1 229)

Coriolanus has followed his own inner conviction to arrive at his present
position. He has despised the common humanity of others, and by
implication that within himself; he has 'grown from man to dragon'. This
image occurred previously in Act four, scene one, when Coriolanus saw
himself alone in his banishment 'like to a lonely dragon that his fen/Makes
fear'd and talk'd of more than seen.' As Rossiter has pointed out, this
allegory of any political idealist continues with the hero feeling some
resurgence of human feelings, throwing away the game he has won and
ending his life in ruin, 'as if a man were author of himself/And knew no
other kin'. It is the final recognition of his 'other kin' which will release the
imprisoned spirit of Coriolanus.

96 5 4 16 'So did he me; and he no more . . .'
This speech of Menenius is, like much else he says, rather studied, courtly
and ornate in its heavy use of metaphor. Notice the contrast with Sicinius,
who, although he has been rebuffed by Coriolanus, offers no criticism or
condemnation of him. The irony of this conversation between Menenius and
Sicinius – if we can call so one-sided an exchange a conversation – is that the
audience already know that Coriolanus has relented. This is a device which
Shakespeare used skilfully, and which here points up the narrow character
of Menenius. An additional irony is of Coriolanus being characterized still as
a 'dragon', when he is about to fall from 'god', through 'traitor' to 'boy'.

95/98	Conflict
95/0	Creatures
86/97	Menenius
77/98	Tribunes

97 5 4 21 'He/ sits in his state . . .'
Menenius is suggesting that Coriolanus has become a figure like Alexander
the Great (356–323 BC), who conquered Greece, Egypt and the Persian
Empire, founded Alexandria and was King of Macedon. Interestingly in this
context, Alexander began his reign surrounded by enemies, and had to put
down rebellion in his own kingdom.

78/98	Domination
89/98	Power
95/99	Coriolanus
96/0	Menenius

Menenius goes on to liken Coriolanus to a god-like figure, distanced from
humankind. About a dozen lines further on, he comments that the gods will

not now 'be good unto us', because in banishing Coriolanus, 'we respected not them'. This deification of Coriolanus continues a theme which runs through the play and which draws upon a range of imagery, from animals to ships.

---

98 5 6 87 'Ay, traitor, Martius!'

Aufidius uses Coriolanus's previous name, and will not grant him the use of the 'stol'n name'. It is interesting that this refusal is a mirror of that of the tribunes when they also condemned Martius as a traitor. Would you say that the motives for the two refusals are the same? Consider how far you could agree that the tribunes act out of a mean-minded refusal to accept the sacrifices of Caius Martius, whilst Aufidius gloats that he has finally toppled Coriolanus the god from his throne. How far are both self-satisfied and vindictive examples of the resentment small men sometimes feel for greatness in others?

96/99	Conflict
94/0	Dissembling
97/99	Domination
97/99	Power
95/99	Virtue
88/0	Voices
94/0	Aufidius
96/0	Tribunes

The hero's names change with the times – he is Martius, Coriolanus, consul, traitor, god, and nothing, but he cannot change into the different roles which people cast him in. Some critics have felt that it is this calling upon Coriolanus to do too many contradictory things which actually destroys him; others have felt that his unchanging personality simply cannot adjust to a world in which the traits which thrust him to greatness are no longer needed. Your own view must be coloured by how far you see Coriolanus as having a fixed character. Certainly he is slow to bend, but is he wholly inflexible?

In Plutarch this scene occurs in Antium, but for fairly obvious dramatic reasons Shakespeare set it in Corioles, thus allowing Aufidius the powerful use of the name-identity association in the play, with which he batters at the very foundation of his enemy's character:

> Ay, Martius, Caius Martius! Dost thou think
> I'll grace thee with that robbery, thy stol'n name
> Coriolanus, in Corioles?

---

99 5 6 101 'Name not the god, thou boy of tears!'

Coriolanus appeals to Mars in frantic disbelief at being accused of treason and cowardice by Aufidius; the reply which Aufidius makes provokes two of the most quoted passages in this play: 'Measureless liar, thou hast made my heart/Too great for what contains it. "Boy"! O slave!'; and later 'Cut me to pieces, Volsces, men and lads, . . .'.

93/0	Child
98/100	Conflict
98/0	Domination
98/0	Power
67/0	Service
90/0	State
98/100	Virtue
97/100	Coriolanus

What often excites critical interest in both these speeches is the way Coriolanus seems to take extreme exception to the word 'boy'. Some critics, perhaps concentrating on the Freudian mother-son relationship they detect in the play, have proposed a betrayed sexual relationship between Aufidius and Coriolanus to explain the latter's outrage. Others have proposed the arguably less extreme view that he has been shocked into recognizing one of the uncomfortable facts of his life. Critics of the latter persuasion point out that Coriolanus's constant, and they argue almost incoherent, repetition of 'boy' is because he at last sees that he has been his mother's 'boy' all along; he has been manipulated by her against his better judgement. This has brought him to his present impasse. His penultimate speech therefore is defiant, tragic and poignant:

> If you have writ your annals true, 'tis there,
> That like an eagle in a dove-cote, I
> Flutter'd your Volscians in Corioles.
> Alone I did it. Boy!

It is perhaps also another bitter irony that Coriolanus should be accused of being a boy, with its Elizabethan overtones of being effeminate, at the moment when he has reached his greatest emotional maturity and has shown the most compassionate humanity.

If you feel drawn towards the critical view of *Coriolanus* which accords it more satire than tragedy, then you may see the end of the hero, not as the moving death of a great tragic hero, but rather the deserved result of his supreme folly. In this, you might feel that Shakespeare's reason for making it difficult for the audience to sympathize with Coriolanus reflects the author's reluctance to arouse sympathy for a character whom he wishes to deride. However, you may feel that the character of Coriolanus was meant to represent the self-destructive essence of Roman civilization, with the plebeians representing the dangers of democracy, and that Shakespeare was therefore expounding to his audience a moral or political lesson. In support of this argument would be the observation that *Coriolanus* has little 'human interest', and no sub-plot.

Alternatively, you may feel that this scene is the culmination of the 'childhood' idea which runs throughout the play. Perhaps we see the tragedy of a man whose mother has finally released his love for her, and the victory of Aufidius over Coriolanus is the victory of the smaller man over the greater. Certainly it is a victory won with tears alone, as Aufidius three times proclaims:

> At a few drops of women's rheum, which are
> As cheap as lies, he sold the blood and labour
> Of our great action. Therefore shall he die,
>
> (5 6 46)

> He has betray'd your business, and given up,
> For certain drops of salt, your city Rome,
> I say 'your city', to his wife and mother;
>
> (5 6 92)

> . . . but at his nurse's tears
> He whin'd and roar'd away your victory,
> That pages blush'd at him, and men of heart
> Look'd wond'ring each at others.
>
> (5 6 97)

It is in this context that the word 'boy' proves explosive, and Coriolanus is killed by the people. Given this interpretation, Coriolanus has returned to his deepest loyalty – to his mother. He has learned to accept that strength can be weakness, and that the acceptance of one's own weakness can be the supreme act of strength. So, as Aufidius put it, 'strengths by strengths do fail'. Perhaps Shakespeare's theme is that even the strongest must learn to kneel, to accept the humanity in themselves and therefore in others. Perhaps, after all, Volumnia was right at the start of the second scene in Act three:

> You might have been enough the man you are,
> With striving less to be so: . . .

100 5 6 150 'Trail your steel pikes. . . .'
This closing vignette is a mirror image of that at the start of the play; but where this is in poetry, the former was in prose; the play opens with tumult and ends in reflection; the steel pikes which are raised at the start are now brought low. To what extent has Coriolanus become a mirror image of himself at the start of the play also?

99/0   Conflict
99/0   Virtue
99/0   Coriolanus

Consider to what extent Volumnia's wishes for her son have been granted. Has her willingness 'to let him seek danger where he was like to find fame' resulted in what she hoped for: 'his good report'? Or have her fears been realized – did Coriolanus 'voluptuously surfeit out of action', that is, abandon action for a quiet life or, put another way, forsake the brutal honour gained from killing for other, more tender, human values?

The play is riddled with irony: Coriolanus the Roman hero dies out of Rome; adored by his mother he dies in dishonour; in seeking to have 'good report' of him she gets him killed. Are you able to feel that Coriolanus can have the 'noble memory' Aufidius promises? Was the death of Coriolanus unjust?

Political checklist

Several characters hold civic positions in *Coriolanus* which we might find unfamiliar today, and therefore confusing. Below is a brief outline of each of the offices mentioned in the play, which it might be useful to consult until the terminology is thoroughly familiar to you.

Patricians
These were a small group of wealthy landowners who controlled the government by appointing some of their number as Consuls. The patricians (magistrates) dominated the composition of the Senate and were an hereditary aristocracy. In the early days of Rome they held virtually all the higher offices, and they created and established the laws of the land.

Consul
One of the two patricians who were nominated by the Senate to control civil and military affairs with the assistance of the Senate. They jointly exercised the highest authority in Rome and were formally elected by the citizenry after their nomination by the Senate. A rough equivalent today might be the President of the United States. After holding the office for one year, the Consuls were prohibited from further service.

Senate
This was the legislative council of Rome and was originally the council of the kings of all the smaller states. The Senate was the highest authority in Republican Rome in matters of law, religion and civil life.

Plebeians
The common people of ancient Rome.

Tribune
An officer elected by the plebeians to protect their interests. Originally there were two of these officers, but later there were ten. Tradition has it that in 494 BC the plebeians marched out of Rome and threatened the patricians that they would set up their own town further up the Tiber. As a compromise, the tribunes came into being.

The patricians were never altogether happy with the tribunes, for the latter had wide-ranging powers, which included powerful rights of veto, and so they constantly worked to get rid of them. Notice that Coriolanus (a patrician) is banished from Rome by the tribunes, not the Senate. The tribunes saw themselves as the defenders of the people's rights.

Forum
In ancient Italy this was an open space, serving as a marketplace and the centre of public business. The main Forum of ancient Rome was situated between the Capitoline and Palatine Hills.

Aedile
A patrician of ancient Rome who was in charge of public works, games, buildings, and roads.

Lictor
These officials preceded the Roman magistrates on official occasions carrying fasces – one or more bundles of rods, which often had an axe-head projecting – as a symbol of the magistrates' power. They were a kind of ceremonial mace-bearer.

Chronology

1497	John Cabot discovers Newfoundland.
1498	Vasco da Gama at Calicut: the sea route to India found.
1499	Amerigo Vespucci charts part of the South American coast.
1509	Accession of Henry VIII.
1513	Machiavelli writes *The Prince*. Balboa discovers the Pacific South Sea.
1517	Martin Luther nails up his Ninety-five Theses. Beginning of the Reformation.
1519	Magellan begins first circumnavigation of the world. Death of Leonardo da Vinci.
1521	Mexico conquered by Hernando Cortes.
1532	Henry VIII divorces Catherine of Aragon. Peru conquered by Francisco Pizarro.
1533	Henry excommunicated, marries Anne Boleyn. Birth of Elizabeth I. Ivan IV (the Terrible) becomes Czar of Russia.
1534	Formal breach between England and Rome (Acts of Succession and Supremacy).
1535	Execution of Sir Thomas More.
1536-9	Dissolution of Monasteries.
1540	Francisco de Coronado begins exploration in North America.
1543	Death of Copernicus; his *De Revolutionibus orbum coelestium* published.
1547	Death of Henry VIII. Accession of Edward VI.
1553	Death of Edward VI. Accession of Mary Tudor.
1554	Mary marries Philip of Spain. Birth of Raleigh.
1558	Death of Mary. Accession of Elizabeth I.
1564	**Birth of Shakespeare**. Birth of Marlowe.
1568	Mary Queen of Scots flees to England.
1570	Excommunication of Elizabeth by the Pope, who declares her deposed.
1571	Birth of Johann Kepler.
1572	Birth of Donne. Birth of Jonson.
1576	The Theatre is built.
1577	Drake begins voyage around world (returns 1580).
1582	Raleigh becomes favourite of Elizabeth I. Gregorian Calendar introduced by Pope Gregory XIII.
1586	Trial of Mary Queen of Scots.
1587	Drake attacks Cadiz. Execution of Mary Queen of Scots.
1588	Defeat of Spanish Armada.
1592	*The Comedy of Errors, Henry VI*.
1593	Plague in London. Theatres closed. *Venus and Adonis, Richard III, The Two Gentlemen of Verona*.
1594	*The Rape of Lucrece, The Taming of the Shrew, Titus Andronicus*.
1595	Raleigh's first voyage to Guyana. *Love's Labour's Lost, A Midsummer Night's Dream, Richard II, Romeo and Juliet*.
1596	*King John, The Merchant of Venice*.
1597	*Henry IV*, Parts 1 and 2.
1598	*Much Ado About Nothing*.
1599	The Globe Theatre opened – Shakespeare a principal shareholder. *As You Like It, Henry V, Julius Caesar*.
1600	*Merry Wives of Windsor, Twelfth Night*.
1601	*Hamlet*.
1602	*All's Well That Ends Well, Troilus and Cressida*.
1603	Death of Elizabeth. Accession of James I. Raleigh found guilty of high treason and imprisoned in the Tower. Lord Chamberlain's Men become the King's Men.
1604	Peace with Spain. *Measure for Measure, Othello*.

1605   Gunpowder Plot. *King Lear.*
1606   *Macbeth.*
1607   *Antony and Cleopatra, Timon of Athens.* Virginia colonized by London company – Jamestown founded.
1608   *Coriolanus, Pericles.* Quebec founded by Champlain.
1609   *Cymbeline, Sonnets.*
1610   *The Winter's Tale.* Kepler's work on Planetary Motion.
1611   *The Tempest.* Authorized (King James) Version of the Bible.
1613   *Henry VIII.* Globe Theatre burned.
1614   Napier publishes his explanation of Logarithms.
1616   **Death of Shakespeare.** Inquisition investigates Galileo's astronomy.
1617   Raleigh sails on last voyage to Guyana.
1618   Bohemian Revolt begins Thirty Years' War. Execution of Raleigh.
1620   Voyage of *Mayflower.* Pilgrim Fathers settle in New England.
1623   Shakespeare's works (First Folio) published by his friends.
1625   Death of James I. Accession of Charles I. Charles marries Henrietta Maria (sister of Louis XIII of France). War with Spain.
1628   Harvey publishes his work on the circulation of the blood.
1629   Parliament dissolved. Personal rule of Charles I begins.
1630   Peace with Spain.
1642   Civil War begins.

Bibliography

Before all else, please make the effort to go and see the play, if at all possible. There is absolutely no substitute for this and a very real extra benefit can be gained from seeing several productions done by different companies or directors. The effort you put into this particular activity will repay itself many times over and, possibly unlike reading criticisms, it has the added benefit of being fun.

The literature on Shakespeare is vast, and it is pointless to expect that you could read everything. You will not even be able to read all that there is on any one play. The following short list of ten titles is therefore bound to be hopelessly inadequate for the student who wishes to become really expert in the detailed background of literary criticism which exists for Coriolanus.

Your teachers, assessors and the examination boards will all hope, however, that you have delved into at least some of the criticisms which are available, and the following is therefore a 'taster' to indicate some of the range of different approaches to Coriolanus which critics and scholars have used, to encourage you to explore for yourself. At appropriate points in the commentary I have referred to some of these authors, amongst others, so that you might get some idea of what these approaches contribute to a study of the play. If you have access to a large library you should make a point of browsing through the many other alternative criticisms which are available – the librarians will help you if you get stuck and, if in real doubt, will frequently have amongst their number someone who may be able to offer you detailed advice.

Ralph Berry *The Shakespearian Metaphor* (Macmillan, 1978).
P. A. Jorgensen *Shakespeare's Coriolanus – Elizabethan Soldier* (Modern Language Association of America, 1949).
Wilson Knight *The Imperial Theme* (OUP, 1931).
M. Levith *What's in Shakespeare's Names* (George Allen & Unwin, 1978).
Michael Long *The Unnatural Scene* (Methuen, 1976).
J. E. Phillips (Ed) *Twentieth Century Interpretations of Coriolanus* (Spectrum, 1970).
M. N. Proser *The Heroic Image in Five Shakespearian Tragedies* (Princeton University Press, 1965).
J. L. Simmons *Shakespeare's Pagan World – The Roman Tragedies* (University of Virginia Press, 1973).
C. Spurgeon *Shakespeare's Imagery and What it Tells Us* (Cambridge University Press, 1935).

Essay writing and examinations

It ought to be obvious to any candidate when the question paper is finally opened and the questions eagerly scanned for those which they can answer, that the **question** is what the actual examination paper is all about! The candidate who thinks the examination is about answers looking for questions is sadly misinformed and woefully prepared.

The following notes were written after reviewing examiners' comments on English literature examinations over a five-year period, and covering most of the examining boards in the United Kingdom. They are revealing in the comments which they have in common.

Answering the question

Discuss . . .
Write an essay on the significance of . . .
Consider the portrayal . . . and their significance . . .
Discuss the ways in which . . .
In what senses do you regard . . . ?
Discuss the portrayal . . . with this criticism in mind . . .
Consider the importance of . . .
Identify some of the main themes . . . which theme do you
consider is treated most effectively?
Do you agree?
To what extent do you consider . . .
Can you defend . . . ?
Discuss the role . . .
Consider this comment in relation to . . .
Discuss with reference to . . .

Examinations requiring candidates to answer questions which incorporate such phrases as are illustrated above (taken at random from one board's paper) are actually saying to the candidate, 'We want to know what you think'.

However, it is not as simple as this. They are also saying, 'We want to know what you think about the question we have set you in **this** paper which is lying on the desk in front of you. We want you to read the question carefully, not just part of it but all of it. We then want you to answer that question, not just part of it, but all of it.'

Perhaps this all seems obvious, but the evidence of the examiners' reports suggests that many candidates are failing to gain marks because they have not done what the questions demand of them. Examiners also require that candidates should know **how** to discuss and consider, and that they are aware of the literary implications of what the examiners are asking them to do.

The candidates first task then is not merely to read the question to be answered, but to study it: to analyse its requirements, hold those requirements at the front of the mind and to prepare the answer accordingly.

Preparation of the answer is essential if you are to ensure balance, development and continuity. As you write your answer, constantly refresh your mind as to the question's requirements. When you have finished your answer, check that it actually answers all the question.

As part of your preparation, take a pen to the question and underline all key words. Jot down on your answer paper all the points the question requires you to answer. As you deal with them in your answer, tick them off.

Do not copy out the question or any quoted extract from the text which may be part of the question. It may give you a psychological satisfaction – a false sense of security that you are doing something useful – you are not. An activity such as this is a complete waste of time.

If you go into the examination room and are not thoroughly acquainted with your texts, then no amount of irrelevant detail, quotation, or comment will gain you any marks at all.

Organize your time

Know the requirements of your examination: how many questions you must do and from which sections; the total time allowed; the allocation of marks to questions and sub-sections; and organize your time accordingly. Unanswered questions gain no marks whatsoever! An extra long essay will not magically increase the number of marks allocated to that question by the examiners. Care and balance in your use of the time allowed is essential if you are to do yourself and the examination paper justice.

What are the examiners looking for?

First of all, examiners require an answer to the question. It has already been said at length above, but bears repetition.

Whilst you must have a very detailed knowledge of your texts, the examiners are concerned not to test that knowledge, but your ability to make use of it. They are looking for the candidate who has the ability to read a text carefully, closely and thoughtfully and demonstrate a reaction to the text in the examination room. 'The candidate who thinks, and can be seen to think, in the examination room, will always be well rewarded. A sense of mind in action is a central criterion.'

The examiners are not looking for what your teacher, or study guide thinks, but what you think and feel about the text you have studied in relation to the question you are answering. The personal response is important, but that does not mean they are looking for you to provide the unique insight into the text which has evaded every critic to date. They do expect you to engage your mind with the text and question and give your considered reaction.

It is not the function of this guide to replace your teacher, whose response to your essays will be your best guide as to how they need improving. However, they will not be sitting at your elbow in the examination room, so do ensure you take note of what is said in the classroom, and of the comments made above.

General points to note

1 Please learn how to use the possessive apostrophe.
2 Spell the names of characters and authors correctly.
3 Colloquialisms and slang terms, for example 'over the top', 'gaga', 'with it', 'got his act together', merely demonstrate a looseness of thought and expression which is inappropriate for a literature examination.
4 Ensure you have and know how to use an appropriate literary vocabulary. Concepts such as character, drama, narrative, technique, satire, cartoon, farce, comedy, presentation, tragedy, structure, comic, conclusion, diction, tone, symbol, theme, image, plot, irony etc. should not cause you problems.
   Do also note that a mechanical use of these terms without commenting on their effect or function is usually a waste of your time.
5 Where quotation is called for, make it apt and brief. Quotations do not explain themselves. It is up to you, having used them, to point out why and what purpose they serve in relation to your answer. Learn how to incorporate brief quotations into your own prose, and if they are too long to be incorporated, set them out properly.
6 Do not substitute long pieces of narration or paraphrase for the specific analysis which a question calls for: the examiners will already have a close acquaintance with the text.
   If a question does require you to paraphrase do note that it must be in modern English, with the details, tense and person of the original preserved.